HOUR OF THE MANGO BLACK MOON

BOOKS BY LAURENCE LIEBERMAN

POETRY

Hour of the Mango Black Moon

Flight from the Mother Stone (2000)

The Regatta in the Skies: Selected Long Poems (1999)

Compass of the Dying (1998)

Dark Songs: Slave House and Synagogue (1996)

The St. Kitts Monkey Feuds (1995)

New and Selected Poems: 1962-92 (1993)

The Creole Mephistopheles (1989)

The Mural of Wakeful Sleep (1985)

Eros at the World Kite Pageant (1983)

God's Measurements (1980)

The Osprey Suicides (1973)

The Unblinding (1968)

CRITICISM

Beyond the Muse of Memory: Essays on Contemporary American Poets (1995)

Unassigned Frequencies: American Poetry in Review (1977)

The Achievement of James Dickey (1968)

HOUR OF THE MANGO BLACK MOON

LAURENCE LIEBERMAN

PEEPAL TREE

First published in Great Britain in 2004
Peepal Tree Press Ltd
17 King's Avenue
Leeds LS6 1QS
England

© Laurence Lieberman 2004

ISBN 1-900715-93-7

ACKNOWLEDGMENTS

The author expresses his gratitude to the editors of the following magazines, in which some of the poems collected here first appeared: THE AMERICAN POETRY REVIEW: "Breath from the Mouths of Gloves", "Fable of Sky-borne Bananas"; BOULEVARD: "The Baxter Street Waltz", "The Grandeur of Foot Souls"; THE CARIBBEAN WRITER: "Mapping the Sargasso City" and "Magus with Reverse Bananas"; THE CHARITON REVIEW: "Aerial Geographies", "Whip Tail of the One-eyed Chief"; THE COLORADO REVIEW: "Requiem with Trumpeting Elephants", "Peas for Eldorado"; DENVER QUARTERLY: "School for Pancaking"; FIVE POINTS: "The Maverick Hatter"; THE KENYON REVIEW: "Crush into these Blakk Feet"; RIVER STYX: "A Taino's Burbly Hereafter"; SEWANEE REVIEW: "When the Waters Returned"; SHENANDOAH: "Soil Eyes", "Hour of Three Black Suns"; SOUTHERN REVIEW: "The Neophyte", "Madonna with Pumpkin"; THE WORLD'S BEST POETRY online, Summer 2003, ed. Harvey Roth: "Mapping the Sargasso City", "Requiem with Trumpeting Elephants", "The Maverick Hatter", "School for Pancaking", "When the Waters Returned", "The Baxter Street Waltz", "Crush into these Blakk Feet", "The Neophyte", and "Madonna with Pumpkin".

Thanks to the Center for Advanced Study and the Fellows in a Second Discipline Program at the University of Illinois for creative writing grants, which supported the completion of this book.

Very special thanks to Stanley Greaves and Therese Hadchity for their generous help and guidance.

CONTENTS

III.   RAS ISHI: SOIL EYES

PAINTINGS

for my wife, Binnie

I. STANLEY GREAVES:
The Maverick Hatter

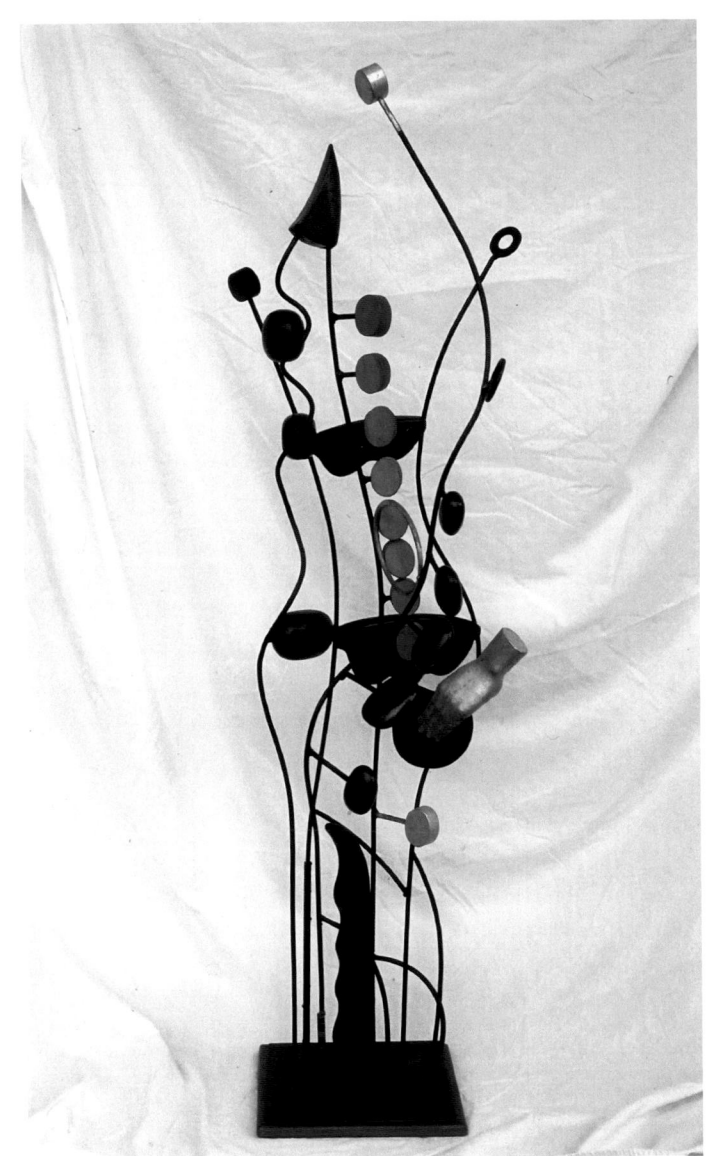

Stanley Greaves, *Peas for El Dorado*, 1993

PEAS FOR ELDORADO

Passing into the entryway, we
   sidestep to avoid
      a mixed-media standing sculpture, wood
         and metal: it could be
      sentry guarding the house front portal. Greet my *Peas*
for Eldorado, says Stanley, the frame rising

              to our waists – no
           higher... Small wood spheres,
        of slightly differing sizes, hang
      suspended by thin wires in an ascending
    pattern from the base to topmost level. The few
      wires, near-invisible, strive
        to give buoyant
         illusion that the balls
      are weightless balloons. Or afloat
         in space
    like a scattering of planets in the heavens.
    But the greenish tint evokes the title.
    They're unpodded peas, which
        have been strewn

upwards by the golden hand below,
   its fingers outspread
      as if it has just completed the toss
         releasing the chain
      of balls spiraling above. The hand, which glitters
like a dress spangled with sequins (a metal

oxide glaze,
transparent, flares the hand's
gold sheen), seems to be reaching –
perhaps endlessly – for some lost glory.
But trusting the hint of wry title, we may ask
why that mindful hand would choose
to fling peas
after the fabled king
of immense wealth, or the affluent
great city
bearing his name – Eldorado. Those many pilgrim
seekers for the mythic city and its vast
gold stores may well have courted
some elusive

Spirit of the remote hideaway
town, by offering
up reward or ransom to the keepers
of the flame. And what
better lure than a handful of island-fresh produce?
Sweet peas gathered from fresh-plucked pods

and then hurled
into the wistful vortex –
hundreds of years of those hapless
explorers… The gilded hand, wire-framed
at bottom center, invokes the sculptor's homeland:
Guyana. The king, himself
reputedly born
and raised in Colombia,
traveled to Guyana's interior
to found

his gold-mine blessed city. In his prime, he'd
celebrate sunrise, each day without fail,
by coating his whole body
with a crusted

layer of pure gold flecks — then lazily
scrubbed and rinsed it off
in the sea as the sun's fiery disk broke
free of horizon... How well
our sculptor knows that Fate, alas, shall bode ill
for the searchers. Over these many centuries,

no scores! But
when did that ever halt
voracious quest of those gold-
blinded Europeans, tireless raveners?
Gold hand, that faithful partner, tosses its peas —
sprinkling of prayers & blessings —
to aid the lost
pursuers, no helps ever
good enough. For some, to chase
the phantom
may be its own reward; that hope perhaps survives
their deaths, while these peas keep spinning
in flight — moons or satellites
that eternally

circle mother planets... Sir Walter
Raleigh, his appetite
for limitless wealth roused by first glimpse
of Guyana's rain forest
interior, sent his eldest son to fetch the treasure,
the lad and his entourage soon drowned in the pitiless

quick whirlpools
of the raging Essequibo
River. Raleigh – at last a broken
spirit – returned to his surprise
beheading at the hands of King James I: rebuke
and penalty for his purported
abuse of Spanish
colonists… Klaus Kinski,
as Aguirra, shaking his vengeful
fist at
deep-forest Cosmos, proclaimed himself *The Wrath
of God*: he, and he alone, become the last
survivor of his expeditionary
river crew,

all others succumbing to the blizzard
of fleet native arrows,
his Queen Intended – that blond teen-age beauty
Aguirra had wrested
from her parents' clutch – struck by a late feathered
shaft; the mad despot, catching eye glints aflash

like fools' gold
between shore trees, still
wildly fantasizing he must soon
inherit Eldorado's great promised trove
of riches… Sun breaks free from cloud cover, now
streaks through Stanley's open door,
kindling anew
the hand's glittery
metal-ore pulsation. Light beams
play about
those little spheres, the dance of flung peas ever
luring the next sorry chasers after woods-
sequestered hidden lucre… *Lost
City of Gold*.

AFTER TWO PAINTINGS BY STANLEY GREAVES

1.   MADONNA WITH PUMPKIN

For all her
nude allure, seated on the velvety plush
of an arm chair,
and her cool cast of features (slight insuck
of cheeks and flat-to-scalp ears), she exudes a never-
been-touched, never-kissed
frailty… What dizzying clash between her slim legs
enticingly spread apart –
one propped on the ottoman before her –
and the wide yellow pumpkin,
perched, heavily, in her lap. It could be a ribbed balloon

or child's toy
pumpkin, her pose so relaxed, unstrained.
But the orange fruit's
ripply vertical bulges impose its true mass
and solidity on the viewer's eye. How does she bring
it off? The placid calm.
No gymnast or acrobat, a brooding Madonna bared!
Not for one moment may we
suppose her flesh to be other than soft.
Tender. If she be transfixed,
in hypnotic trance, her autonomous steely nerve-cord surge

might bolster
the massive squat oval with outsize lift.
Her push could appear
effortless, as now. But the Madonna's sidelong
glance is alert. Wide awake. Full access of attention.
No lapse of conscious grip
seems possible… Still puzzling over her guise
of comfort, I examine
the wooden mallet at rest on the floor
beside her upraised foreleg,
a shapely green leaf growing from its handle, upborne high

on its stem
like the firm uptilt of her breasts. Leaf
and breasts seem to share
a secret – they know the calculus of lift, lift:
the talent to carry mass as if it's weightless, to defy
gravity with skill of spring.
Bounce. To leap in the wind as a spirit leaps. Breasts
and lone leaf signal each
other, ready to perform a duet, partners
in the world just outside
our painting – or in the Time just after this event occurs.

The portrait
hints some next place waiting to unfold –
whenever the painter
lays down his brush, that magic wand. The pumpkin,
too, partakes of erasure of mass – saving the Madonna's
legs. A rescue, no less.
To her right, the vertical cannon stands guard.
It would protect her,
one of the legion of cannons transferred
from old forts and propped
upright at street corners to insulate house walls from auto

bumpers: cushions
to repel car blows. (This cannon was lifted,
the artist discloses,
from the corner of Rugby and Tenth.) A black grackle,
fearless, is poised on the rim of cannon barrel, one leg
raised over the shaft
agape. He whiles away his time, may never leave
her side. We know he fakes
aloofness, wary that the pumpkin – if left
to its own mood swings – shall
crush her legs. This we'd abhor. But the dark eye forbids it.

2. THE NEOPHYTE

Young upstart, a budding socialite!
Now he's practicing
at dress-up. Shirtless, his blue tie is pre-
knotted around his neck, in rehearsal
for the debutante's ball.
He's getting up nerve to try on
his white jacket
suspended in space   hovering high
upon a black hanger   attached nowhere.

But his eyes betray he's anxious,
frozen in mid-dress
stasis. Why can't he move? Perhaps he fears
the jacket's too long. Or too short.
And he dreads the cost
of one more trip to the tailor...
Stanley treats
me to glimpses of his inner studio
secrets, unveiled. In revising mode today,

he takes in a sleeve and shortens white
jacket's lower hem.
As you can see, I'm tailoring this garment,
he says, playful as he mock-sweeps
his empty right hand
to and fro across the upborne
coat's bottom,
working his fingers as if snapping
a large scissors at frayed cloth borders.

His whimsy is mixed with fond respect –
                             or outright envy
                 perhaps – for the tradesman's deep engagement
with streetfolks on an hourly basis.
                                    I sense how he must miss
               that verve of human contact, feels
                    too sequestered
                              by his chosen work. So he vows to make
his art *speak to the many* – if more to woo

them to his ideas than be gasping
                             at beauties… He muses,
                  now, over this sweet young fellow who wants
to be a big-up. But he's shy, *lone wolf*
                             stuck in a lovesick tussle
               with nature: Gardening his métier.
                    He's poised on
                              the verge of dating, but what a gulf
he faces – it chokes him up… *How can we know*

all this from viewing your portrait?,
                    I ask… *My secret,*
               only I need know, his reply. *The model's*
character may peep out at you, by
                             subtle turns of color
                  or shades of light – but I must
                    know his Being
                              to the core, up and down, to give him
a vivid pulse. I, alone, must see far past

the exterior I paint, and X-ray
               his body in mind's
       eye, to show him true to feel ... The line-up
of buttons on his jacket looks oddly
                    asymmetric, at first glance.
       Ah, they're beetles trailing little
           brown legs, not
                    threads adangle: no proof of careless
sewing as it had appeared. Such detail-work

challenges the looker to view close,
                    to search for meaning
       beyond the normal scene – its *lull of everyday*.
There the vision starts. But it sweeps,
               by infinitesimal slow shifts,
       into the Occult, always just a wee
           half-step around
                    the corner from usualness… Baby
beetles, in trios, adorn the sleeve ends.

A wing-folded grackle, lifesize, nestles
               in the left high pocket,
       mimicking a handkerchief, its tail dangling
out like a black shoelace. Iridescent
                    blacks of tail and wing
       feathers seem to flutter as if –
       at any moment –
                    our hanky bird may pop out, take flight
over the expertly cuffed and knife-edge-creased

black trousers hung by two chalk-white pins
from the taut clothesline
overhead, that thin rope ominous horizon
stretching from painting East to West…
Will the neophyte conquer
his timidity, and unsnap those
trouser legs
from above – which seem to loom too far
in the distance, remote, beyond the lad's reach?…

THE BAXTER STREET WALTZ

Fillets, even whole fish, seem to crackle & flake
before they touch her griddle. She
flips them so fast,
like pancakes – we wonder
how they grew those golden brown thin crusts.
Sizzle & pop
in air?... Rotund she stands before us, at helm
of the longest line: Mrs. Baxter,
countess of fast order
cooks. Her rate

of grilled crispy
turnover is double time. She takes
her name from the fish-fry hullabaloo road,
the place for huge crowds when a big catch
of jack or mackerel hits shore. And we wonder how word
spreads so fast, or why
Baxter Street has a corner on the market. They wait
in such long rows
to be served, each one choosing
his or her favorite fry cook,
no matter which line may be shortest. And while they wait, jokes

Stanley Greaves, *Mrs. Baxter*, 1992

or gaming fever passes the time. Some throw dice
for sizeable bets. Others set up
instant foldout
tables for dominoes.
If enough money changes hands, the crowd
thins – some losers
left too impoverished to pay for fish... Today,
she wears a novel costume. It's
her magic cook show, more
dream antics

than gobblers' fete.
    A loose over-garment is tied around
    her waist, smock or apron to catch the fast grease
spatter. Her chef hat's a tall white turban, spot-
lessly clean, normal looking except for two green-and-yellow
       fish tails shooting upwards
from the top in all directions, as if rooted there
and growing like fungus
      or wild mushrooms. And she clasps
a large black skillet in one hand,
centered over red hot embers of a charcoal fire. The wide oil blot

spread in the pan assumes a familiar shape, for its
an aerial sky view of Barbados.
Four dominoes
are spaced out, evenly,
over the blot, usurping the place of fish.
Her whimsical look
shows pleasure in the work. If the dominoes fry
is a joke, she's not in on it.
Business-as-usual, that's
her demeanor.

A sparkly red
      snapper, so fresh its scales glisten,
       is stood upright on its tail, balanced over
that low work table beside her flaming
grill; a bulky super-sharp chef's knife, blade downward,
         hovers on its fine point
next to the snapper, its mate for length and breadth.
Rivets in the knife's
      handle stare back at tall fish's
goggly cold eye. *Perhaps knife*
and fish are having a dance, they're fond partners, says Stanley.

      Three peppers – one green, two red: that ideal combo
          for a fish fry – are strung, loosely,
              around the knife
             handle. *It makes a proper*
        necklace, as well, for Madame Blade. Nearby
          squats a large whole
     lime, it too stood on end. What else could we wish
       for cooking snapper? But today,
         she sautés dominoes… In
          her free hand,

she lifts a money
　　bill with a pencil poked through it.
　　The paper currency is stamped *ZERO*, issued
by *EVERYMAN'S BANK*. She is taking charge
of the whole country, silhouetted as the oil spill laid
　　　　out flat in her black pan.
She would run the economy with that zero dollar
budget; slot machine
　　　　bars and casinos abound, no
revenue left for the basics.
The Baxter Street feeders, in long lines for the famous fish fry,

　　　　　　would rather play for high stakes than be feasted in
　　　　　　　　queenly style. Hence, they exchange
　　　　　　　　　　domino or dice-
　　　　　　　　　dot eyes for the snapper's
　　　　　unblinking goggle-bulge eye. The roadside food
　　　　　　　　　　stalls are displaced
　　　　by the lottery, our cook's bad memory, and pencil
　　　　　　　　eyes poked in the dollar... *Waltzing*
　　　　　　　　　　fish and knife run away
　　　　　　　　　　　with the moon.

THE MAVERICK HATTER
(Georgetown, Guyana)

Stabroek Market, busy center
of a spider's web, is the preferred kinsfolk meeting place
        for this whole sprawled country.
            All crisscrossing paths, threads of travel,
merge and interlock here. The tradesman, taking heart from confluence
            of types to whom he sells his wares,
labors to transmute
        his body cells – blood, nerves
            & brains – into the atomic make-up of his product.

                                The vendor, so
                    to say, comes to vend his lifeblood
            reconstituted as hat felts. Who he is
    is what he does, his very being engendered as hats. (The trade
                    that you do's the *pith* of you.)
In his calm eyes, a lull of steadiness – not stupor. But finding
                        the way. A dignity. He's the best
            hat magus in town and knows it. This faith
                            gives him magic...
            Six hats are piled, one upon another. A little tower
                        of hats. Six brims

        perhaps a full inch apart. The foot-
high column is propped on a polelike slender branch, a large
        short-stemmed leaf growing
            sideways from the shoot: it starts just under
the hats. They appear to float a little, as if air runnels flutter
                between them though they seem to touch,
to fit into each other.
        Subtle currents may be flowing
            around the bowler tops and brims, an emanation

26

Stanley Greaves, *Hatman*, 1992

from life streams
of the plant rooted below. (But it's
the center of town, the market: whatever
can be growing here?) The man's left hand, hidden behind
that heaped-up row of hats,
seems to conjure buoyancy, while life-flow of serums in the branch
firing the leaf supple on its stem
may delicately influence the hats – they, too,
imbibing elixir.
Or perhaps they drink directly from the hatman's arm
vessels: a veiled

set of fingers working its sleights
behind the scene on view... The seventh hat is balanced,
absurdly, on one edge –
its vertical brim poised at right angles
over the tower of six. This one blatant oddity comes leaping out
at the viewer, and slowly leads
our eyes to all other
abnormal details: the live-branch
hat rack, the inverted tin cup atilt on the stick

of sugar cane
that he grasps with his right hand –
square cup bobbing alongside his squarish
jaw and forehead tucked in the brightly sunlit eighth hat
(the other seven all shadowed,
here and there); and lastly, the two chicken eggs queerly stacked
one atop the other – propped sideways
on the window sill: the window shape itself
an exact square,
black hole framed in cabin wall to the vendor's left.
The pair of eggs

nestle just above that seventh hat
on end, it too unwaveringly still: both white marvels –
        upper egg shell, vertical
                hat brim – maintained in perfect stasis
like a spinning top. The placid unsmiling visage of the hatman gives
                        no clue to formula of his tricks,
his secrets borne lightly
        by the level set of his dark jaw
                and precise V of his black neck line geometrically

                                zigzagged into
                        collar of his cream-white shirtjac.
                An oval aperture, the fabric head gap
        in the magic upright hat stood-on-end, warmly coalesces
                        with the oval eggs piled
overhead in a squat little figure eight. The jest of balancing acts
                                conveys his affection for passers-by.
                Yes, he wants to catch our attention and lure
                                us to buy wares;
                but more to the point, he's a bold dreamer – a merchant
                                of brain caressers,

        so he would fit hat size and shape
to the wearer's fantasy. His hats would guide us to blessed
        choices in love and work.
                The right hat brim tipped and curled just so
may win the truest mate, lady companion to our heart. A hat seller
                who can balance eggs that way, and keep
wide brims gaily standing
        on edge all day, may be clairvoyant.
                He purveys more than a drab product. The right hat's

lining may feed
messages to the brain within... Shaman
we can trust! To surmise from the cane stalk
he grasps, he must hail from long line of farm folk, planters
and pickers of sugar crops.
To master his trade as hat connoisseur, he took early lessons
from working the land, from tilling
the soil. One leg in the country, one leg
in small towns,
his hats were nurtured by his family's green thumb.
They never grew

on the tree whose leafy branch props
them up. But those sweetly rounded bowl tops may take buxom
curves from farm-grown fruit; hat
brims drawing their pliant edge – holding upturn
for countless bends and snapbacks – from a sapling's trusty flections.
The hatman instills lessons into hanks
of our hair, both curly
and straight with equal magnetic
zip: he tinkers and attunes the wholecloth of our dreams.

29

ACUITY

This woven mix of childhood mementos,
    in oils, is drawn from thirties and forties working class
Georgetown, his father's prime.
    The exact particulars of keepsakes and sweet
    normal daily objects are cherished, but rearranged. A fantasy
of side-by-side cavortings in geometric shapes
and niceties of design...

    The eye is teased and tossed about, idly
    enticed from locus A to locus B. But the one most intense
acuity, that focal center we
    come back to again and again, is the razor blade
    edge just touching the fragile bottom skin of a fresh-picked
cherry, its stem still in place above. We know
the sharp blade will soon cleave

    lone ripe fruit, mid left, that dramatic
    pairing fitted on a deep-space square of Magrittelike
sky. The dark story of cherry
    split, vivid slicing-to-come, is sure tribute
    to Dali's razor cutting of live eyeball in the Bunuel film,
itself a memory keepsake. This tool! Can it be
that secret implement which boy

    Greaves – forbidden to carry a penknife
    by his mother – kept in his trousers pocket for snatched
moments of playful whittling?
    Woodcraft an early passion of our sculptor-
    to-be... Below the blade, we find a twirled fragment of rope,
likewise subject to the razor's cutting edge:
some leftover helix of twine

from the toolkit of his father, expert
rope-mender, no one faster or more adept at difficult
splicing and tying of exotic
knots. Four *Edge-a-Boy* biscuits, great favorites
of the street kids in his child time, claim the middle zone
here, arranged in a vertical lineup of squares
turned sideways like diamonds

and layered one over the other, the top
biscuit divided into black and yellow wedge halves.
This central row of four-sided
shapes is balanced by the clever pyramid
of six balls stacked in the upper left corner, held in place
by two nails, driven into the shelf top
at both ends: nail brackets

the one proof that our six piled rounds are,
in fact, spheres. Three-dimensional. Metal brads age well,
so perfectly free of any trace
of the old bends or curves, we'd never surmise
they are two salvaged from the copious supply that had filled
a deep drawer in his father's toolbox, all
faulty nails. The child spent

many a rainy afternoon unbending them
into exact straight lengths to appease his sire… Telltale
pencil, leaning at an acute
angle to the horizontal shelf that holds
small pyramid of balls, is signed by the artist, as if itself
the very wand that conjured – and thereby
fused – the whole composition.

DOOR STOOP AMOURS

                        Mr. Knife has just come
              to try his luck with the local
              belle, tall elegant Ms. Okra standing upright
in the well-lit doorway
              on her one pointy toe. She's
                  dressed to the brow, and maybe waggles
                            ever-so-slightly
                                      those natural long ruffles
                  of her dress – a full body suit
                  topped by her stemlike head… He's come acourting,
and thus salutes her
              with his vertical white bone
                  handle. He leans a little to the left,
        casually propped

                                      on his blade edge vanishing
              from view, just below the four-step
              approach to her front entryway. Perhaps he leans
on a cane, one hand
        cupped stylishly over his hip –
              the angle of his tilt exhales confident
                        aura. No more
                                  than his bone top & uppermost
              blade are displayed here… Her stance
              is coy, mildly flirtatious, no sign that she'll ever
rebuff him. Her figure –
        framed in the arch and brightly
              lit by house interior – casts a long shadow
        down those steps.

The black eclipsed sun, white-
haloed, is poised above the open door
outswung on wide hinges to her left, its two tiers
of shut jalousies
hiding all but the exposed feet
(three-toed chicken legs?) of the clandestine
brash third party,
eavesdropper on the droll scene
of courtship. What chance, we might ask,
would the scrawny pale interloper have in combat vying
with the stately knife
for Ms. Okra's love?... We are left
with questions of scale, which oddly varies, here
and there. Tallish

svelte Okra and her suitor
are of similar height, we suppose –
though half of his blade leg slinks from view. Closed
door in the divided arch-
way to her right is a half slice
of brown toast, which is adorned with two buttons
lined up as befits
a sporty dinner jacket,
in place of the usual knocker
or metal ornaments... Perhaps Sir Knife pays his visit,
instead, to offer
to perform one of his chivalrous
popular rites – the spreading of jam or butter on
her door of toast.

FABLE OF MISMATCHED PAIRS

The block of steps,
   so often employed to mount a horse
in the plantation era,
   is divided into two rows –
three high steps
on one side, five shallow gradations down the other.
   Both sets are adorned with a chessboard
pattern of black & white squares. Black sun, upper
left, must emit
   strong light, since the riding boot on top-
   most step casts a dark shadow,
and the oval mouth

      at shoe's high rim
   is brightly lit. A second boot, at right
angles to the first, is
   gargantuan – perhaps quadruple
size. Which boot
is normal scale, which a prodigy of construction?
   The huge boot, settled on grey floor
behind the step block, would crush the platform
if any wearer
   tried to climb it. What breed of human
   could fill this boot? An old
plantation backra, or

overseer, no boot
                too large for his burly stomp. The workers –
both cane field minions and
                cotton pickers – had better stand
clear, or get
trampled underfoot. The vertical nail, atilt at lower
                right, is the only item in scale with
immense boot – but the architect's signature is engraved
upon the nail,
                so it's special. In a class of its own.
                No true gauge of boot sizes,
then. And we mustn't

                forget, wide size
                swings are the norm here. We note several
out-of-scale pairings. Two
                handsaws, two cups, two limes. One
large, one small,
                of each. And again, there are tall steps on the block's
                right side, half-high steps on the left.
Ah, half-sizing gives us a going ratio, except for one
massive boot, mostly
                offstage: its upper half, or more, towers
                out of sight, over the edge.
If the boot story

toys with politics
of colonial days, the plantation saga,
the handsaws come down
to toolcraft of our present
day; while cups
and limes are shrunk tiny enough to serve as twin pawns
on the chessboard: two sizes, each, for
those varying board squares, two stair rows. Surely
we are invited
to partake of dialogue between mismatched
pairs. And we may learn to live
with disproportion,

inequities, size
or color clash -- for every day, we grow
abler to tolerate
those questions without answers
in worlds outside
Art... But *Plantation Boots* cheers us on to play our board
games, and seek a logarithm that can bridge
wide size gaps on the stage set framed between a Black
Sun and signature
nail, in opposite corners. Blessedly, just
one of each. *Would a Gulliver take*
heart from size freeze?

Stanley Greaves, *Mr. Facial, No. 2*, 1992

SCHOOL FOR PANCAKING

A fresh cucumber patch covers the black
                model's left eye. That
          necklace of lettuce clumps and tomato wedges
       loops under his whitely cream-puffed ears
              and jaw, all those face parts
        smeared with zany makeup alike,
          except for untouched
              dark circles around his right eye
and pinkish-wet lips. One secret recipe,

          comprised of food
      elixirs, is protected by the bureau of patents
       (punishable by hefty fines for leaks) –
note that trademark tattoo
        inscribed on an exposed eyelid… All natural
fruit and nut extracts quickly surpass the surgeon's
       cutting blade: Ponce de Leon, in the form of herbs ground
     by mortar in pestle.
A drop sample reveals to tongue-tip-
        mind tinctures of camphor,
     almonds, honey, chamomile, pine nuts, lemon –
all fused in the cream-white face potion…
        At portrait top floats the dosage: four
   or five lines, some words crossed out,
     others in bold caps

underlined for emphasis. Letters tilting
backwards or forwards –
clownish alphabets as in graffiti – divulge
the exotic blend for a *facial*: inside
dope on the rare formula
which restores youth better than
surgical facelift.
Chemical alchemies! But patrons
must donate huge tuition fees to attend

this cosmetology workshop.
At first glance, he looks like a masked reveler
disguised for a carnival pantomime.
We have only the cream-
smudged face to go by, no hat or costume frills
in view, but the gummy texture of face balm soon
looms false to spirit of *MAS*, high carnival… *This must
be how we truly see
ourselves*, says Stanley. *Odd inversion
of Al Jolson's white man
in Black Face: bootblack's ink smeared from ear
to ear*. He'd seen a beautician's poster ad
promising ultimate skin bleach, *whiteout*
of inbred pigments, perhaps, if thick
marshmallow face cream

be plastered each dawn to soak for an hour
                        before work. Skin pores
                would quaff deep draughts for the ideal buildup
        over months, years, of such pancakings…
                        We find *MR. FACIAL, NO.2*
        printed in monumental bold letters
                under the face portrait,
                        as in a huge billboard display.
        Roadside poster art. It's a fond tribute

                to the artist's father
        who loved to draft giant characters on public signs,
                one of the many dirt-wage ad hoc vocations
        he plied to scrounge extra
                        revenues for family upkeep… The face unguent
    for sale, thick as a French potage, boasts strictly
                organic makeup, as itemized on jar labels. But why choose
        mere sprinkles of food
extracts and herb juices tossed in the brew
                to transform our skins – cheeks,
        jowls and ears? Wholes slabs or wedges of fresh produce
may be strewn upon the body direct, both
                        as jewels in a necklace and mask parts… *Our face*
        shall become the mask, creamy second life
        squirted from a tube.

MAPPING THE SARGASSO CITY

We pore over an urban setting,
any seaside town in the islands. Do parts
of buildings stand for wholes,
the looker's eye to fill in missing walls, roofs,
floor sections? The damages
do not plead for rescue – by *The Red Cross*, or teams
of paramedics.
No post-mortem of earthquake, nor war zone
aftermath: rather, this scene
could pass for
a poorly assembled stage set. Who could be fooled
by these tilted
facades? Teetery balcony or gable? Both
standing walls are cracked, zigzag chunks
missing, here and there. What a sham! False fronts
are looming at the audience of watchers. We viewers,
observers of this locale,

are a given. Some attempt to put a face
on this run-down godforsaken excuse for a townscape
has been slapped together.
But who is trying to put one over on us, pray
tell? And who are we, anyhow, to be fooled so easily? The main
presiding consciousness, hardly a cognitive
being, is the black dog –

all four paws balanced on telephone
wires, he surveys the scene. We can almost
hear him snarl, while he commands
the high right quadrant. A black sun, upper left.

Stanley Greaves, *Prologue: There's a Meeting Here Tonight* (left panel detail), 1994

Is this, too, a façade —
if colorless – for our own solar body? Or perhaps
a Black Hole
that has mistakenly wandered into this bleak
near-human earth site: a gaping
mouthlike void
from outer space that, however toothless, seems to
have gobbled up
the missing puzzle parts of this city (no limit,
say the *astro cognoscenti*, to how much free-
floating matter those galactic throats can swallow).
More likely, it's a black sun, since the sky color varies
from sunset purple below

the phone lines and modulates gradually
upwards to twilight crimson on the roof tops. Wide black sun,
then, is the inept stage
crafter's façade... Two forked tree limbs growing
through oval gap in the only church wall left standing. Did they poke
fat hole in the mortar-loosened bricks, driving
the long diagonal crack

down to the foundations? We look
again. The tree branches support the wall
frame, after all – they may be sole
bulwark that props up the lone fragment of church
remaining erect. Natures's
futile attempt to come to the church's rescue, when
stone mason and
parishioners, alike, seem to have abandoned
that crumbling edifice to Time
& the elements...

41

Jagged segment that survives is a small fragment
of the structure's
former glory, revealing little more substance
than a billboard. Hence, it best mirrors
hollow rites of the clergy, and those dwindling
flocks of the faithful. A large bell, dangling its frayed
rope, is still intact, though

tilted off center in the wall-top arch.
Five black dogs, the same breed as that phone wire strutter,
idly circle the church
courtyard. If they were humans, they'd strike a pose –
shifty-eyed and cunning – of some gang of thugs or vandals plotting
urban sabotage. How little of value survives,
but they're intent on wreckage,

more from boredom, perhaps, than evil
plans. The dogs are us, as we soon discern.
Ourselves in canine skins, clicking
our four paws on the coarse gravel – thin disguise!
Attitude shows through. It's
identity here. If we forget who we are, we plunge
into *The Void*.
That doggy part of our psyche takes over.
Our absence in the setting,
by default,
is portrayed as black mutts ... The dilapidated
church and nearby
tenement house, missing a left wall and oblong
patches of roof, are ignored by the dog
team; they're too preoccupied, too blindly driven
planning a political rally. That second-story room,
exposed through some lost wall

42

panels, is open to view. A bed, shakily
standing on three legs, displays a feces-stained mattress
half-fallen, which disgorges
pink stufffings from one corner. But the focal center
of the ramshackle apartment's layout, odd shock detail that most
amazes our eye, is the child's orange rubber ball
stalled on the bedroom floor

above the bent frame of rollaway cot.
The floor is sloped at a sharp angle. That ball
should be twirling down the incline –
from all the signs of dereliction in this gutter lowlife
place, the Law of Gravity
must still be in effect. Stationary ball is the key
to our whole off-
center sleazy town vista, since everything
in this mock-human village hangs
at a standstill,
frozen to a halt. A pall has fallen upon the bosses,
mostly absent
Ministers of State: all progress is blocked,
no civic balls can get rolling down their
steep floor tilts… In upper right corner, beyond
those loyal stalwarts – two telephone poles – we make out
a lone full-sailed schooner,

triple-masted, no more than a mile distant
from shore. Ballooning tiers of sail leave no doubt the vessel
must be pushing seawards
against heavy wave-tossed swells and fighting off
sub-surface drag, visible dark patches of thick Sargassum whirling
and tugging back on the hull. This miniature
replica of Wide Sargasso

Sea, like immovable floor-stuck ball,
is emblem of the sticky quagmire gumming up
all human affairs in its hopeless
entanglement, as if that web of dense vines, tubers
and rubbery tentacles has
trapped our ensigns of progress in its whirlpool dead-
lock of clinging
weedy arms. But the fiercely plodding schooner,
whose many levels of inflated sail
cloths surge
in concert, will cut through watery morass – the upward
heft of bow sure
sign that she's knifing a pathway to reckless
whitecapped abandon of open sea: Arielesque,
her undaunted facing into the brunt of all weathers, her
four-hundred-year history of surviving battles with a gamut
of warships… Best of the pirate clans

swore by this sleek-hulled, right-and-ready
old soldier to stay the full course. Likewise did those warring
colonial factions employ
such hardy vessels as privateer craft to haul bands
of mercenaries – launching many an unrebuffed surprise assault on crews
better armed, or more numerous… Check out the logs
of her swashbuckler captains.

Stanley Greaves, *The Annunciation*, 1993

HOUR OF THREE BLACK SUNS

Pre-election weeks…
Days, maybe. You can feel the heat of its near
approach. Offstage, camera bulbs
are flashing –
the candidate to be announced and his helper
garishly overlit
by the photo team. Urban street scene?
He grasps two mikes, a metal shaft
in each outstretched hand: one black, the other
silver, thick electric cords trailing offscreen
in either direction. Upraised,

that round black mike
is a near-twin to the black sun
hovering just above it, both spheres eerily matched
with his right eye-glass blackened over
(opaque sun shade: he can see out, nobody can see in). Left-side

normal eyepiece is clear, transparent.
One eye shows, the other's hid. He must be a man
of two minds, two voices. One blind eye,
one seeing eye, perhaps he shall vouch for two sides
on every issue. And two answers
to any question. He stands, posed for the snapshots, hip-

deep in an oil drum:
former mail cargo box, onetime carrier of gifts
from their North American family
or friends,
turned garbage pail. The trash bin, twice recycled,
begins its third
life as go-cart for speedy removal

and transport of candidates from one
political waystation to the next. His cool
                aplomb, that lax poise: is he primed to give a long-
        winded double-dealing speech?

Does he suppose he's
settled in for a long rally,
        to be feted with mob hoopla and applause, little
        suspecting he will be swooped afar –
        at any moment – by his frumpy helpmate? The lady cane field

                        worker, armed with a sawed-off sugar
stick tucked in her fist like a war club (weapon
            at the ready), grasps the bright handle
        of trolley cart on which he's perched. And whisked away,
                in mid phrase, he'll be. Or even
        before he opens his mouth to spout his demagogic harangue.

            Rashly, he assumes
her support, taking for granted the common folk
                    will vote for him – this streetwise
                        bloke, his garb
            an odd mix of semiformal and sporty, baseball cap
                spun to one side
        revealing those red-and-white bars
                        over royal blue flashy sports coat
    (his loyalties must be secretly promised,
                sold out, to American backers)....The black dog
            looking athwart from the street –

he's subversive rabble
waiting for the first chance to riot,
        spoilers of any planned rally... *The Annunciation*.
        We suppose his party's prime candidate
        will be *announced* today – perhaps he? – with startling revelations

46

of high Biblical import. His lady
field-hand associate might yet be chief sponsor,
            poised on the verge of launching him
with dazzling intro to the crowd. But suspiciously,
            he two-fistedly clutches both
mikes, perhaps fearing that she controls his pull-cart

            trolley... Most colors
of the scene are squeezed into the narrow darker
                    band of the spectrum: blacks, blues,
                        greys. Black
            hands and faces, ink-black malevolent doggy fur,
                white-and-grey-striped
        dress shirt buttoned up to white collar
                        beneath lapels of the blue jacket,
    lower coat tails flared-out, sportily, above
                    the man's hips. So jarring, then, is the contrast
        of few shiny gold plate details.

Gold belt buckle, gold
rims of his thin-metal-frame glasses,
        row of four gold shirt buttons (from collar to waist),
        and half-hid glittery gold cuff links
        peering out from under his blue coat sleeves. That tiny arsenal

                        of jeweled flecks, if near unobtrusive
at first glance, signal his likely drift to bribes
                from wealthy client States – should he be
            elected: hence, his proneness to stuff his own pockets
                    with gilded rewards. All frills
    or perks would top his priorities. And the farm lady's

47

traditional work
attire hints she and most commoners would be kept
                            in their place – no hope of rising above
                        bleak lowly
            station. His grip on those two ball-shaped voice amps
                    is set off against
        her holding fast to trolley bar and cane
                            stalk: four palms clamped shut. By sudden
        onset, with no warning, they may fly off
                        in opposite directions. No need to ask which pair
            of hands will hold sway. Never

can he match – much less
resist – the powerful tugs and hefts
        of her muscular leg calves, field-toughened for exit
    fury... Those power cables, we surmise,
    are affixed to huge wood speakers beyond our view: street dance

                            calypso boom boxes on briefest loan
to the campaign. He hovers, as if dandled
                from above on marionette strings, few
        puppet lines doubling as electric cords... Meanwhile,
                    that black dog – half concealed
behind the podium backboard (so close to the candidate

            and his dazed partner
they cast shadows that very nearly touch the brims
                        of their hats) – attends with sinister
                        glare. Looming
            in back of the dog stands the House of State, its
            windows darkened.
        Nobody's home. The house wall, half lit
                    by street lamps, seems remote – aloof
        to proceedings of the next block. The night's
                main event, set up to misfire before it can start...
        This photo is over-exposed.

48

Stanley Greaves, *Banana Manna #2*, 1995

FABLE OF SKY-BORNE BANANAS

Stoic and serene. All the rage of island farmers, due to banana
          wars with the United States
and Britain, is becalmed. Held under wraps. All future
    banana crops will be lowered to them
on ropes from another dimension, much like the five-banana clump
      here affixed
    to the vertical length of cord. Enchanted food
     of divine origin, *Manna*
        delivered
     by the gods – has it dropped
   from the sky, shunted on a direct pipeline from
      Heaven to Earth?
This farmer is holy man or seer, having less to do with planting
   or agriculture than conjuring, secretly,
with those higher powers. Three disjunct ropes arrive
    and depart, as if randomly,
from margins of this setting. But we feel they're all connected

               behind the scenes,
           glimpsed segments of the one
         life line. Banana sage turns his back
        to us, half of his black face revealed in
      profile, the other half hid in his droopy red hat
        which flops down over his eye and ear.
              Another rope
           is tied to his red hat, knotted
       twice, one time on the hat's peak, again
               at the far end.
Two long banners of hat cloth go trailing overhead
        like loose ends of a scarf flying off
           canvas to the left. A third
              rope is looped

around the man's chest, tucked just under the arms of his elegant
    long coat. Two kitchen pots –
the rope knotted around their handles – are laid out flat,
    face down on the man's back, small aluminum
soup pan above the wide black skillet. Both pots cast dark shadows
    on the lower coat
which is split, stylishly, down the middle. A spoon,
    handle end pointing downward,
      is fitted
through button hole of the coat's
side pocket. The spoon – at the ready for use – rides
    on the chef's right hip.
He's less farmer than Master Cook, perhaps? ... The rope length bearing
    a stalk of bananas, that gift from cloud-dappled
sky, drops from painting upper margin, its extension loop-
    twisted in a figure eight.
One bulky three-toothed iron key, tied to the rope bottom, nearly touches

            the low border,
        Manna rope almost as long
      as portrait is tall. While we brood
     over the august figure of purple-coated
man, who gestures commandingly with his right hand
     toward the banana cluster, his open-
       fingered palm
    seems suspiciously close in size
and color to the five-banana-spread darkly
        silhouetted
above the cloud-ruffly backdrop (that local idiom,
    a hand of bananas, ringing in our ears).
     Now his cool passion seizes us!
       All three ropes

are fatefully interconnected. They keep signaling to a dimension
        outside the visible cosmos,
    as if referring to another space and time zone where
        they originate – their exterior source –
    which feeds them to us but remains remote, just out of our reach.
        And the crux
        of the drama that shapes our lives may reside
        in this adjacent, but unseen,
            netherworld.
        There all the rope tag ends meet,
    come together, whatever in us may seem to be
        at loose ends here.
That trio of ropes, both serviceable and gamy for their variety
    of knots, pay tribute to the artist's father:
a gifted rope mender, one of his many ad hoc vocations…
        Somehow we sense that the key
which floats beneath the strung-up bananas could unlock our passage

                                to the second-
                        sight realm, if we but knew
                    how to make it work for us. The key
                looms close over the sea wall, a wide shelf
            below the man's stance: familiar platform for ritual
                    daybreak offerings to divinity – all
                                holy spirits.
                    But the magenta haze that dreamily
            borders the oblong white cottonball cloudlets
                            hints moment
        of late twilight. The brief magical hiatus between
            sunset and dusk. The man, it would seem,
                    performs a shamanistic rite;
                            his extended

51

hand and the five-fingered stalk are mates, both black with a purply
glaze. Bananas and hand hold
converse, a duet for the audience of little clouds.
Transfixed, a choir of mute watchers,
they loll and linger. The man has summoned the arrival of a special
order shipment
of bananas, rope-dangled from the firmament.
Product of the Empyrean.
Revealed,
signed & logged in. No ordinary
soil-begotten fruit, it is *Manna*, food for angels,
borrowed on loan or
purchased at what high cost to replace lost market share of banana
exports. This godsend windfall string of fruit
is the second chance market. In lieu of those big shipments
freighter-hauled abroad, *Manna*
is code work for *Bananabis*... The chef hangs up his pans, hidden behind

his back. In place
of edible food, mind blowers.
The spoon in his coat pocket button-
hole is all-purpose implement. It serves up
sugar for coffee, both former saving crops (as cloud
balls recall the cotton trade of yester-
year), or white
powder for snorting. Too much to read
into the one vertical spoon? Perhaps. But spoon
and key seem
adjunct pair of mates, one juxtaposed to the other,
so close they nearly touch; they may signal
each other, as do the two hands
paired above. Spoon

52

is a key, the one utensil that parades longest history, companion
        to the heart of the painter.
    How he loves spoons! To draw one is to celebrate all.
        For the early Chinese dynasties, bowl
    and spoon were the all-purpose serving combo. The spoon, in *Manna*,
        may forecast
    transfer – for survival – from one lost industry
        or livelihood, so to say,
            to the next…
        All colors of the portrait, but one,
        are low-keyed and quiet, held to a narrow spectrum
            of blues, purples,
    greys, black skin, white clouds, dull unburnished silver of spoon
        and tin-grey soup pan. But so torrid and eye-
    affronting is the hat's deep swatch of scarlet, it belongs
        to another world. The shock
of contrast keeps dragging the viewer's focus to the high left corner,

                    red wind-blown
                hat tails flying upwards,
            taking us up and away from visible
        setting into the unseeable stratosphere, just
    one short mind jump beyond. As all lines in a technical
            drawing in perspective slope to a distant
                vanishing point,
            so do the lovely visible elements
    of this work converge upon an off-canvas zone
                    where our riddles
    would all be solved (and all rope segments do finally
            intertwine), if we could but leap past
            the barrier – the poverties
                of dumb good sight.

53

MAGUS WITH REVERSE BANANAS

Are they freaks, pranks
played by nature on the poorest small-scale
banana farmer? Or did
his sly attempts
to cross-fertilize
new hybrid banana forms backfire? He holds up a tall
stalk to the light
as if he's proud
to display his handiwork. And no regrets!
His dreamy smile is proof.
We wonder how those
five bananas could grow

backwards on the clumps, stem ends
flaring outwards, pointy banana tips queerly joined
to that cluster rim. The Magus, no mere carnival trickster,
blithely harvests
his banana crops and sells to the public.
He still earns his keep, sustains a modest living for his family,
but loss of export
sales eats into his profits—of late betrayed

by America's new crunch
on island quotas. Since most U.S. buyers now
favor his Latin rivals,
he turns his hand
to magic — to win back
fair trade. *Reverse Bananas* may hypnotize the middle men,

as new games often lure
wayward children
back to the play yard... His velvety black skin
seems ashimmer with purple
glaze, while the gold
bananas, too, are bathed

in purplish light. It could be
glows of late sunset, pre-dusk maroons swirling
across the strings of fruit and man limbs alike, marrying
grower to his crops
in a new-birth caul of second skin luster.
The colorist, himself a conjuror of arcane states, had come upon
unique shades of purple
in Britain last year. They partook of both earth

and big sky, a mix of sea-
sky and land-sky, colors that lurk and hover
upon horizons. He filed
away that gift
of new tints in a memory
journal of novel hues, and waited to bequeath them a mimic's
afterglow life within
his painted forms.
Others would carry home new shirts, cloaks, scarves,
belts – high fad or fashion
garb – from their trips
abroad. But he, charged

with a slant of fresh eyescape,
    returned from his travels bearing new color power,
        armed with a stockpile of pigments to dress up and costume,
            afresh, his paint kit...
                Stanley's Guyana roots, his childhood and youth
in Georgetown, are transferred to his Magus. Those early daybreak
            offerings on the sea wall –
        gifts to the Gods, the Holy Spirits – engendered

                                    his belief in wide horizon
            as linear springboard for the happy display
                        of marvels. The clothesline,
                here, is best
                        recurrent magic locus.
        Wherever humans reside, from city to farm settings, our laundry
                twines stretch across yards:
                constant turnover
        of hanging garments and motley blend of other rope
                danglers make this *horizon*
            quiver and flutter
                        with human accoutrements –

a favorite site for shaman's
    rituals. The Magus simply extends his right arm
        toward the line, and his palm print or fingerprint whorls
            launch the topsy-
                turvy realignment of things in motion. It's
a highwire dance act. A tightrope walk of objects that commences
            horizontal side-to-side
    struts across the canvas. An airborne ballet

of acrylics… That wide-ribbed
expanded umbrella, capacious as a small parachute,
stands erect on its curved
handle – stationed
in mid line. It cannot
fall. A strong wind and darting rain or pelted hail can shake it,
make its silks flap in tumult,
but never dislodge
or unsettle it from secure handle placement, true
footing on the rope. We sense
this deep aerial
anchorage in taut symmetry

and poise of stance. The fall-proof
mode… A wave movement flows outward from that hand's
least shake, its minimal tremblings, and the cool succession
of balancing feats
resumes. Two candles teeter on the line, one far
to each side of blonde wood of umbrella grip – both upright candles
sporting long wicks curled
like a woman's sexy eyelash. A sapphire-colored

butterfly with crimson wing
margins and pink stripes lolls on one candle's
tall wick, its wings half-opened
on verge of takeoff
or landing, you can't say
which, but in-between state reveals it must be one or the other.
Flux, not stasis… A single
banana is placed
upon the dome of umbrella nylon, its pointy ends
curving upwards – in reverse
of the black fabric's
concave swell (*the Magus*

57

wants to make us laugh, he can do
   funny things without limit: sadly, he cannot win
      those banana wars — but lifts our hearts). Like a scattering
         of smiles, the lovely
            curves feed into each other: candle wicks,
umbrella handle, butterfly wings and phallic arch of long bananas.
         All half-hidden smile lines
      seem to flicker, in happy interplay, up and down

                              length of clothesline… Maestro
         Stanley, twin of the Magus, hums his ardor
                  for this motif as he traces
               invisible curves
                  over the painting's frame
         with his left index finger wand. And so it is we discover — to my
                  delight — we are both southpaws,
               he and I, our wrong
         curves mirror images to everyone else's. I may as well
               team up with the morning's
            passion — surprise line
               swoops and misturned bananas.

Stanley Greaves, *Morning Mangoes*, 1989

HOUR OF THE MANGO BLACK MOON

Years back, he loved to attend
  the sunrise ritual of mango eating in the lagoon
    or bay shallows. If friends or dear ones joined you, splendid.
      But festive and high-
        spirited, he almost preferred to be thrown in
with a random troop of strangers. They were all locals, your country-
      folk, rarely foreigners,
  much less tourists… This ceremony was insider

        practice, dating
    back untold generations. It smacked of
      a *history*, fed on its own instant prattle of lores
        and enigmas. You came
    early, began the jabber before first light,
  and saved the little pouch
      of mangoes or bananas for daybreak.
      As sun rose, you peeled the fruit and lovingly carved rinds
    into fine lacy or jagged patterns
    of ornate design.
      Bestrewn, they would decorate the waters all
about you, and the inventive shapes would
  catch the myriad
        flux of colors in ever-
    shifting light, and keep you gasping at rainbow
      display. The free interchange of talk might vary from
      family anecdote
    to search-and-delve questions about Life
  of the Spirit, its reach
      beyond daily happenstance. Or the fate of ghostly
      Afterlife Beings that roam the earth, and maybe crawl across

these haunted waters in subtle moments
          of eeriest light
               swings. Morning light –that quickchange artist –
          needs to be watched closely, studied and
               sung: above all,

celebrated... The talk between
     friends, or strange first-met partners, might sweep fast
          through all of these phases and then fall into deep hush. Never
               planned. Always chancy.
                    First one, and soon the others, might break out
     into recitation of verse, inspired on-the-spot proverbs, or those free
               flights of oratory.
     We began by speaking in our own voices and tongues,

                         then other voices
               might take possession of our throats, our
                    Souls, for however brief or prolonged a moment...
                         But alas, he'd seen lavish
                    better days ebb. Fond ritual of bolstered
          spirits now lost its magic,
                    as old breed of bathers, waders,
                    first light worshippers, gave way to slovenly ne'er-do-wells.
               They forsook beauty, all reverence
                    for those sublime
                         minutes, and fouled the waters with excess trash.
In years past, the pilgrims of daybreak
          would tidy up
                         after themselves, gathering
          many scraps and skins of fruit that littered their
                    pristine shallows, depositing them all in plastic sacks
                         before they slipped
                    away. Not so, the new generation of mango
pals! Too often, whole weeks

of rotting and putrid leavings, peels layered upon
    peels, effused odors of rank malediction, a gross pestilence
of the scummy surface. Most radiant colors
    would be bleached
        to a no-color off-white, dead fish bellyup
        shades... In *Morning Mangoes*, an elegy
            for lost dawnglow

heyday, the brown woman and man –
  standing in bay water that just covers their knees –
    are entranced. The red pupils of their eyes gleam like miniature
        suns. Their eye whites
            darken to jet black gemstones, the irises yellow
orange, mango-colored. A sharp horizon line bisects their high foreheads.
        An oversize flamy
    semicircle of rising sun forms perfect wide arch

            over their heads,
        a crystalline blend of white and scarlet.
            Curved like a tall rainbow on the horizon, it frames
                their faces. The sea, dark blue
            at the skyline, lightens gradually downwards
    toward their submerged knees
            and forelegs. He holds two red mangoes,
            she two yellows, one in each hand: four ripe fruit, just peeled
    and ready to eat. Each lifts the larger
            toward the other's
                mouth – to offer a bite... A cryptic black oval,
shaped like a gigantic mango, rests
    on the distant sea
                    surface, balanced on end.
        It could be the moon, its color reversed to black
            like the lovers' eye whites, blackened by a mischievous
                sun's alchemy.

A cherry and its wide leaf sprout on curled
stems from his visor cap,
             another stemless leaf grown backward from his neck.
      Her hat, that many-layered pancake of mango skins thick-piled
on her head, long narrow leaves trailing out
             behind her neck
                    like scarf ends… But we mustn't miss the humor
             of their uniquely fashioned plump body
                           parts. Their hands

are rounded melons. Necks, forearms
   and upper arm segments all comic oblongs loosely strung
      together on thread-slim joints like marionettes. Their globular
             limbs are composites
                    of elongated mango shapes. You are what you eat,
   carried to that playful metamorphosis of forms… *He   garbed in yellow*
             bathing suit and red hat
   she   wearing her yellow mango peel headdress   sports

                    three red cherries
         growing from the top of her one piece crimson
             swimsuit   They are both encompassed by floating
                    curlicues of banana
             and mango peels   the water surface woven
      into a mishmash   vivid
                    tapestry of silks… Half-risen sun
             strikes upper layers near the waders' sashaying dark torsos
      with bright streaks of turquoise, gold
             and sparkly orange,
                    buoying their frolicsome arms and shoulders
toward a new light suppleness   *They bob and pitch*
   with puppets' wild spring…

II. RAS AKYEM:
Stick Paramours

EAR MUG HANDLE

By failing light of near-
dusk in the sprawled museum of hotel
    corridor, we settle on bold harried portrait
    of a half-slavish, half-regal
    black head in profile: *King of Spades*. Your eyes glitter

            with memory
        of modeling this compact *bust* (the head and shoulders do
look sculpted, what with knobby
    angular rounds of jawbones, shoulder humps
      and forehead bulges), the issue of two sweet electric
    afternoons of headlong drafting
at the College of Art in Jamaica. Your boon
    apprentice days… Telltale crown of thorns, pulsating, hovers

    over the head. Both solid and misty translucent,
      it eerily floats
        like a halo and signifies his secret kingship.
          His features are twisted
        in pain, eyes blazing with o'erleap of Spirit – less martyr
than survivor. *SPADE* is scrawled twice, above

and below his profile.
A term of insult, racial putdown, *spade*
    now sizzles with hidden fire – a badge of honor.
    He's a top card in the deck. His soul
    trumps out his captors' feeble hearts. But his grossly

widened ear,
                misshapen, is slotted and curved like handle of an earthen-
ware stein. That squarish cast
        to his jaw and forehead reveals the ugly
            pull of ear handle against natural mould of face bones,
        making of him a mere vessel, jug –
or anonymous tumbler dangled from a demijohn
            neck – into which any contents might be poured, forcibly injected,

        allowing no hope to dispel or regurgitate
            same. The fierce tug
                of handle would refashion our snug proportioned
                    skull of the human
                    into its own insentient mate. As before, today's ex-slave
            is frozen in place, gripped by that head

clasp, while the Western
White drunkard-on-power quaffs a bottomless
        brew… The perforated ear looms large. But flame
    in his eyes and dim floating halo –
    that miracle coronet – shall throw off his eardrum bonds.

Ras Akyem, *Scarred*, 1998

BREATH FROM THE MOUTHS OF GLOVES

      Spelled out
    in fading gray letters
across the boxer's midriff are the words *NO FEAR*.
    The same two words,
repeated in bold black letters, are etched below the huge gloves –
    disengaged, weightless and afloat like airships,
    off to the man's right. Muted scarlet flecks and streaks
    of russet stipple
both the glove masses and boxer's abdomen, forearms, right cheek: less

      overt smears
    of blood than historic
map of many wounds over the years that have left
    this man disfigured.
And irreparably *scarred*… The placement of red swirls – both
    on and off his body – bespeak dual scarring,
body and soul alike, one clearly twinned with the other,
    as felt in color
continuum running, unbroken, between flesh, glove leather and backdrop.

      Punch-groggy
    figure of the blurred man
looms up tall, his facial and body auburns oozing
    into those blocks
of resonant light browns at ringside. Bulging its tanned-leather
    sorrel skins, the pair of inflated gloves
seems to be dangled in space. Down-slumped in mid portrait,
    each billowing glove
pouch – as wide as the boxer's whole chest – hovers alongside his shaken

        frame, upborne.
   At lower left, a block
of paint-free canvas, expressive and fierce, gives
    the work a rocking
and dizzying whirl of motion. The spattered halo of white
    spray, emanating upwards from the boxer's
knotty locks of hair, marks out body fluids aspurt –
    sweat, tears, phlegm…
Those head-shaking moves are a spaniel's, drenched with rain, shuddering

      to cast off
   sizable droplets of wet
(the boxer as culture's pet dog). The man's shoulders,
    arms & some glove
parts are bordered in white, his forearms pinned to his sides.
    He could be dazed, taking blows from his opponent,
braced to endure the savage beating (*NO FEAR*), his neck
    stiffly tilted right.
Six wriggly bright threads ascend from the gloves' unlaced mouths agape,

      oval sockets
   where the boxer's hands
have been yanked free. Those undulant silver lines
    are thermal currents,
sweat-dank fumes risen from glove linings, the scarred man's
    life spilling out of them, leaking quenchlessly
above. Fluttery, they seem to mirror those white spurts
    burbling up and away
from his black scalp tangles…We sense time lapse between turbulently

                battered man
            and wide emptied gloves
        buoyant like helium balloons. Both fumy glove
            interiors may retain
        the boxer's essence for years after he doffs them, following
            his last fight. His knuckle creases and palm
        prints burrowed secret tunnels, hairlinefine canals,
            in seamless leather – breath
of memorial scents ever discharging late traces of the life that was.

MOBY AT RINGSIDE

When Akyem recounts the vivid work high
of drafting *MOBY DICK*, he sighs and chants, waving
 his arms overhead to recapture the way
 brush moves drew upon his whole body. All of his wakened
 and subliminal nerve energies —
as rarely before — came into play: no part of him was left

 behind. Every smithereen,
 from my scalp to my toe pads, was swept up by
 paint strokes. *MY ass,*
 too, was on the line.
 He took those blows
 to his own jaws, solar plexus and ribs, the dizzying left
 hooks to his temples.
 His very innards
 churned... Now he's pointing to many graffiti
 alphabets, as uniquely shaped
 and vivid as tattoos.
 POST NO BILLS, etched

 in white and black, at lower
 middle of canvas, is foremost. It signals the viewer's
eye to upper right quadrant, where
 fierce haunted charcoal sketch of the boxer
 is affixed, an overleaf layer on the canvas. It's the forbidden
 BILL, posted in plain
 view — subversive to The Law (the maker, we
 shan't ever forget, is a rebel who flouts all hollow rules, dour laws
 of our State). Or a billboard

flyer promoting the next championship
bout. Or fugitive-on-the-run WANTED poster, as hung
in supermarkets, train stations and bus
depots. Or mug shot of a just-arrested felon. Or slouched
bum in pre-arrest police lineup.
Snapshot? But the style is an artist's dashed-off cartoony

likeness in a sketchpad…
That boxer's stance, in caricature, leads off
the high drama. Charcoal
black ashen face, mask-
shaped, is slunk below
his wide shoulder expanse, as if hung in fatigue or shame, while
dozing for the police
night photographer.
He stands flat-footed, both feet outspread at right
angles, his arms dropped floor-
ward & hugged to his sides.
Dark gloves are plopped

on his thighs, his V of fallen
chin nearly grazing the waist band of his grimy trunks.
We must look close, to observe
that little kingly crown suspended, aslant,
over his head (his Fame, so pale and fleeting)… *MEAT*, perhaps
the most directly
telling of all those graffiti, is scrawled
near left, beside his legs. He's groomed and disposed for butcher's
quarry, his frontal torso

pose a graph for meat segments to be quar-
tered, hacked and carved into all the premium grades
of beef, goat or pork. Then subdivided
and portioned out to the whole flesh-devouring culture... *POST
NO BILLS*. We can own nothing, not
even our homes, personal effects, patch of land on which our

family is perched, and least
of all, our blood-and-bone-bag, mortgaged off
at a cheap welterweight
ringside auction. Bought
& paid for. Everyone's
for sale at marked-down bargain basement prices... *GOLDEN ARMZ*.
The rough-hewn tag end
style lends itself
to many views of graffiti phrases (*brain-teasers*,
he calls them), scattered, here
and there. *BLAKK MARKET*
cuts two ways. The boxer

hints revival of the old
slave trade, for all his glitzy veneer of sports stardom,
buying and selling of Blacks
by Whites at the fight stadium auction block.
Or smugglers doing their under-the-table business. The original
take: streetwise slang...
The swirl of nebulous words, phantom
graffiti, appears at various angles and sizes of script, or Roman Caps.
These *snippets*, he says, should

prompt viewers into guesses at meaning.
We may wish to *connect the dots*, to play at fitting
many scrabble words together – each to each –

all about his canvas, as in solving riddles or crossword
puzzles. Note *TAR BABY*, recurrent
both as white title over the boxer's head and blackly drawn

across the far left, at mid
panel (*JACK JOHNSON* spelled out in white, just
below the boxer sketch,
in counterpoise to *TAR
BABY* above). We recall
sly cunning of Brer Rabbit in his encounters with the fabled
wolf as he struggles
to free himself
from the trap of sticky tar: all four of his paws
are stuck, and so is his face,
but his tongue's shrewd
wiles save him. Muhammad

Ali the one word-savvy boxer
whose gift of the gab helped him to transcend underdog
demeaning of self with Oversoul
rhymster's wit... *SPADE*, upper left. A card-deck
spade, colored dark purple, not black, transmutes the clover
leaf shape to a purple
heart – badge of honor, lifted from slums
to elitist status. The left panel is topped with *BOX 70* in white bold
Roman, the number crossed out

with a right-to-left red smudge: that Champ
poster hung beside a cancelled P.O. Box. Null & void.
At lower right, *MOBY DICK* is scripted
in large black letters... We love the Black Boxer, he lifts
our spirits, but he's *MOBY DICK*
because the money bosses, those Mafia gangsters, chop him up

73

              into meat, blubber, great dark
   oily hunks of whale fresh. The leap from Melville's
       enigma – that unkillable
       giant White Ghost whale –
       to Black Boxer
  whale is a whole continental shift of message along the racial
      fault line. It owes more
      to islanders' long
   history of true whale hunts, or whale butcherings.
        Their piquant memory of taking
    family for a holiday
        to St. Vincent's small

   offshore islands designated
  for whale dismemberment, followed by lusty whale feasts...
Whenever news of those few
  yearly leviathan strikes may spread down-isles
  and up-isles, some hundreds of miles in all Antilles directions,
    it draws the lovers
       of whale carving spectacle and banquets
  alike, from all land tracts – far or near. And today's star harpooners,
    so few they are, know Moby

          lore from Gregory Peck's Ahab fifties
variant... Soon after any new Champ's launching, he's
     stripped of all unique personhood, shrunk
    to human hamburger. Then crowd-tossed ring kill. But despite
    his squandered powers, we look to him
  as ikon. The boxer is White Whale survivor's darkling twin.

A TAINO'S BURBLY HEREAFTER

For nine months in Cuba a Fellow at Instituto
Superior de Arte, he earned his rep as a solitary. Or recluse.
    Too shy to admit his dearth of Spanish, he chilled
out – froze like a deaf mute…

                                    Ras, you must take
        a local lover, his art coach wryly counseled. And yes, post-
                                coital joking
            in bed was a speed course on street slang. Soon after,
                    words and phrases aplenty for all things
came tumbling forth. And he made many fast friends, easily garnered
                                big-hearted welcomes.
                    But the police and ruling class, from Fidel
                        on down, abhorred

    dissent. Even in art. And subversive – albeit
joking or comic – was his métier… To stay out of jail, then,
        he'd have to disguise any sharp caveats at bosses
of the land, keeping elusive

                                        in his least attacks.
    Hatuey was his prize anti-government diatribe, stowed away
                        under Juanita's
            wardrobe, for fear of confiscation and swift arrest
                if he tried to ship the satiric cityscape
home. That work could never squeeze through tight customs, for all
                        his cunning to conceal
                barbs of his acid-tongued theme… Prohibitive
                shortages of color

pigment forced him to improvise novel forms
and paint substitutes. He chose flat board constructions, dense-
textured collages, perhaps many layers thick, rather
than standing sculpture. Half

history, half myth,
was the saga of Hatuey, martyr-saint who became an ikon.
Taino Indian
from Santo Domingo, he risked his life voyaging
to Cuba on a sail-driven raft: brave
messenger, he hoped to warn indigenous tribes that Conquistadores
were coming — too late!
They'd long since arrived, and taken command
of populous shore

settlements. And whoever they didn't massacre,
they cooped up in cages like monkeys, driving the stray pockets
of runaways into deep forest hiding. They converted
many jailed thousands to some

semblance of Catholic
Faith… Promptly arrested Hatuey. Put him on public exhibit
in chains and ankle
irons. Tortured him to renounce his Taino Gods and
convert. He scoffed at all possible wounds,
flogging, mutilation. So they roasted him at the stake — let *that* set
portentous example
for any who'd come after. But those survivor
Indians all claimed

him, if secretly, as their hero. And model.
No surprise, then, he comes down to the present day as rebel
            martyr to the Cuban masses. Thus the ruling powers
have shrunk his noble stature

                                                by plastering labels
        with his stalwart photo on beer bottles, cans, bearing his name
                                    as brand. Ras Akyem's
            collage layers actual mint labels which he peeled whole
                and intact from used bottles he'd collected.
Arranged in semicircles of a great rose shape, the labels half shroud
                                    some touched-up photos
            or portraits of street prostitutes scattered
                    beneath the blossom.

    Fragments of printed words, below and between
the labels (letters often crossed out, as in careless graffiti),
        can be pieced together as variants. *First I was a man.*
And now, I'm a Gold Label brew.

STICK PARAMOURS

I.

Two mantises are having sex – female above
        to the left, stricken male
    lower right:
long lean stick bodies, they could be scrawny
        humans, so little flesh
    on bones
(all but emaciated to a gleam), knobby bumps
        for knees, small elbows
    and shoulder
joints the humanoid giveaway. Or fierce eyes!
        But twiggy mantis segments
    they remain,
as well…
            This moment, they've sprung apart –
        wide space between them,
    a prolonged
coitus. Two skeletons, man and woman sprawled
        across the canvas, four limbs
    contorted
in pain or ecstasy. Primal twist of their arms
        and legs, as in cave drawings,
    petroglyphs,
suggest frenzy of tribal dance leaps. Acute
        bends may be war moves. Swings
    of rage. Love
coupling and your classic battle of the sexes
        blent in the spiraling fury,
    bodies in flux.
Love wails and war cries may intermingle, perhaps
        merge in the wavy voice lines

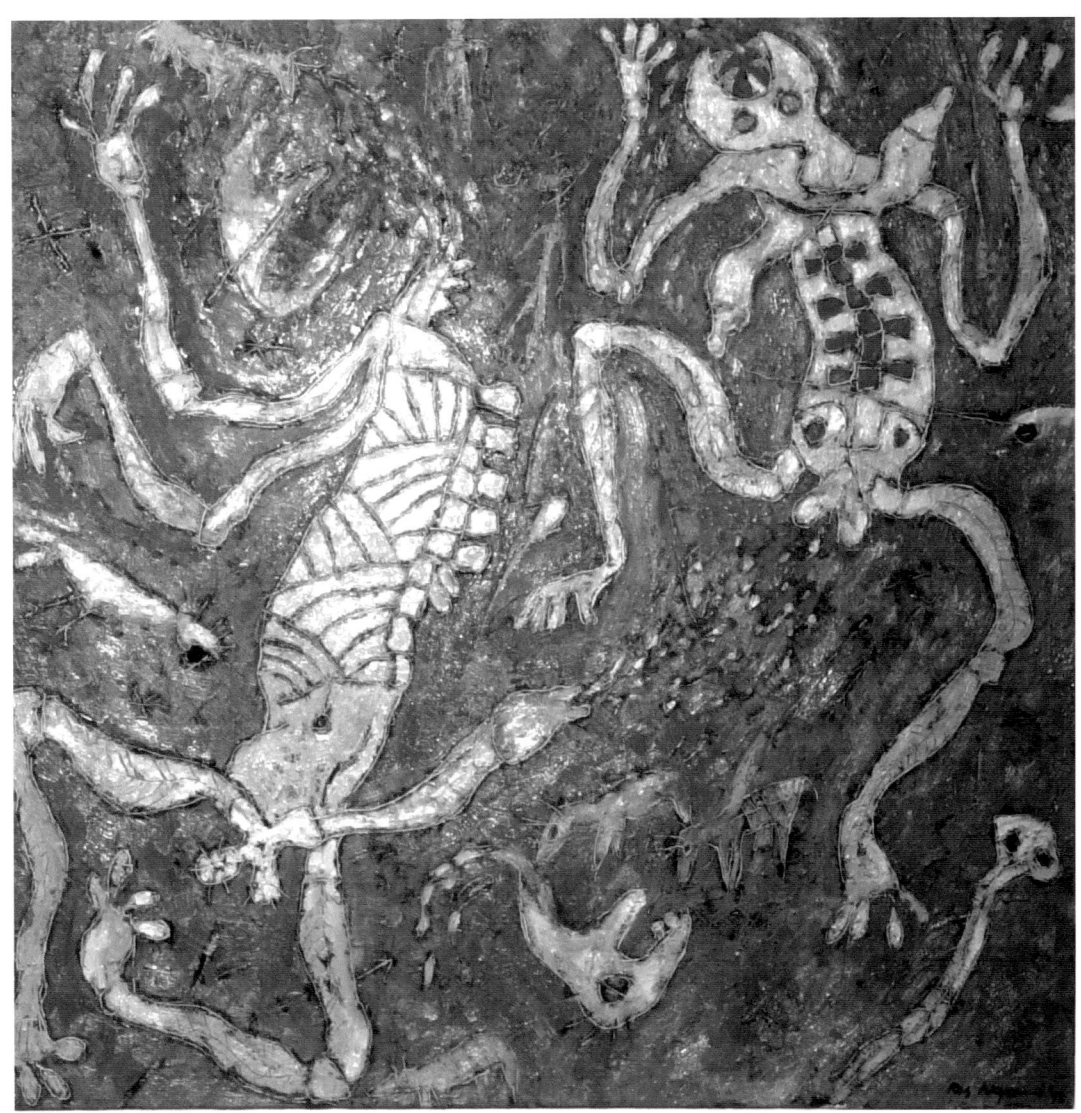

Ras Akyem, *Mantis,* 1995

of graphlike
backdrop. Sound waves or nerve vibrations: who
        can say what those many dim
    line wriggles
transcribe?...
          Two streams of droplets, curving
      awry, are spattered across
   the foreground.
Uppermost, the long trail of semen, tiny sperm
       tails aflicker, here & there,
   in the spray,
tall penis still fully erect and exposed aspurt.
      A second, that short gusher
   thickly oozing
from his neck.
        Ah, she's beheaded him in mid
     coitus, the decapitated skull
   oddly grimacing,
fallen to the ground underfoot, his blood more
       plenteous from severed neck-
   half below
than from above-shoulder spout. His lower body
      still writhes in love spasms,
   oblivious
to the loss of its brain bulb. Headless-chicken
    mode...
       Her glare of conquest
   so evident
in her tilt of brow, we know her secret joy.
     She conceives new life & claws
   her ex-mate's
skull off in one pure moment. A simultaneity.

            *   *   *

Misogynist, they call me.
But I adore women, could never hate a lady. Yet fear
            of the female pervades
this portrait and many other works. *For she is the true*
                predator. Her aggression,
which disguises itself as tenderness, is far more lethal.
                        Sinister, she's the *serpent*
hidden beneath the *wildflower* – more dangerous for being
            unsuspected.
                    The mantises
are us. These stick figure insects – who mingle the passions
                to love & kill so we
cannot tell them apart – lurk in all humans…
                        That day, Akyem
                was seized, yanked by surprise.
These creatures sprang up – as if whole in their scraggly
            misshapen limbs, tubelike
extremities – from thick tactile canvas he employed. Rough
                surface of that medium,
so new to his touch, drew the pair of fierce animal hybrids
                        from his brush. As he daubed
paint into the coarse-grained field, it seemed to spawn
            two slender twist-boned
Beings to answer the firm swish and stroke of his tools…
            Borne of his wrestling
with the *Angel* of plaited textures, they were engendered
                        less from his mind or hand's
fine rapturous sweeps than from that papyrus thick scroll-
            work of crinkly paper.

                    *   *   *

What the source of these grotesque imitation
          humans? Copies
               of ourselves... The tall stick
of our body sprouts branches – necks, shoulders,
          backs & hips
               are extensions of arms & legs,
a reverse of the familiar body orders. He watched
          these person-
               morphs seem to crawl or weave
across his paint swirls in amazement. For all
          resemblance
               to that mantis he'd pored over
in science class texts, boon of his school days,
          their posture
               and bearing on his matted page
expressed a mind of human animals. And he let
          this sorcery
               of dual species draw from him
such hybrid creatures, spun out of our psyches
          as if waiting
               to be discovered by his half-
asleep brush strokes: more found than invented,
          sprung whole
               from the abyss of pre-racial
memory. Their closest kin in the family of seg-
          mented animals
               are scorpions & tarantulas, tail
or hairy limbs poised to inflict their stings.
          But the truer
               brethren may be those wiry
scrawled spiderlings that survive for millennia
          on cave walls,

    thrusting beaks and twirled
claws over the arched wall-to-ceiling murals
   of petroglyphs...
     Color, too, seems primal or
antique – both creatures and sullen backdrop
   they wriggle
     across draw upon the same
narrow band in the spectrum of whole colors:
   all tints, hues,
     of the work moving between
light brown, tan, beige and deeper yellows.
   Paired bodies
     are luminously red-tinged,
as in ocher, while the parts of mandibles &
   curled talons
     appear to be faded sienna,
darkest shades anywhere on sprawl of canvas.
   The shimmering
     desertscape of terrain (vague
demarcation between sky and land) is grainy
   stucco yellow –
     it radiates light of a low
dun sheen...

II.

Long before he takes the plunge
into a new cycle of paintings, Akyem
gestates. He may wander the island outskirts for weeks,
months, exploring chance
nuances in nature and slowly
containing his thrills of discovery, hints
about fine threads
that hold the cosmos together:
those knits & hinges that bridge
all worldly parts of things, until he finds he's dreaming
gummy hookups, the glues
and caulks that cement his daily
bric-a-brac, piece to piece. And he must feel
this great mucilage

of Being has infiltrated the dark
core of his dreamlife before *onsets*,
before he commences the finely cadenced rituals of paint
launchings. He works best
when this glimpsed amalgam roars
into his blood beat – true subject and idea
always snapped up,
discovered, found waiting for him
whole in its own dream-skin, *ripe*,
rather than invented at whim, or concocted by his direct
controlling will... *You'd never*
guess how far into the adventure
and vision of making a paint work I already am
by the time I build

my stretcher of sticks & nails
and pull the canvas across it. Ah,
those innocent tools have a secret life of their own, and I
must keep them pure.
　　　Soon after he applies his first
　　　　　flecks & swirls of paint, the work surges –
　　　　　　　　barreling along,
　　　　　　　　　　　　perhaps halfway to completion.
　　　　When the silhouettes of our two
　　　　　randy stick paramours floated onto the burnished gold haze
of sandy waste landscape,
　　　　　Mantis seemed all-but-finished.
　　　　　　My dream is an engine, Akyem muses. *A train*
　　zooming down the art

　　　　　　　　　　work tracks. It's fully in swing
　　　　　before it pulls the congeries of color
　　　　　streaks & pigments into its vortex… The colors that fed
this erupting vision
　　　　were stolen from the sun-baked
　　　　　surfaces of ruins: that distinct blotchy
　　　　　　　　rude color mix
　　　　　　　　　　　　of old crumbling walls, shattered
　　　　　roofs, jagged cornices, pillars
　　　　　and foundations gave him their patina, their softly pungent
tones of stain & tarnish.
　　　　As he pored over the ruins of old
　　　　　Amerindian stone huts, some chattel houses among them,
　　they prompted in him

a lust to capture their essence.
He'd wandered the vacant semi-desert,
surprised to come upon some gravelly weed-riddled grounds
of a long-abandoned
site, parts of walls still standing,
zigzag margins showing where breaks carved out
hulks of stone.
He cruised these zones by first
light, starting just before dawn,
hoping to study the very earliest layers of glimmer settling
on those grimy pitted
surfaces revealing – at last – the aura
of most oldened color blocks. Arisen like spirits
from the dim shadows!

So tremblingly alone he'd stood,
searching for he knew not what secrets,
who craved a message from this living spectrum of yellow
golds. He kept pondering
fallen blocks, the ravaged home
shards, ignored and forgotten for centuries.
Had they become
invisible, perhaps, to anyone
but himself (how mercilessly
alone, he felt)?… His art was frozen stuck in an old groove.
To free it, he'd muster
his face up close to the telltale
visage of rock, sniffing the crosshatched exterior
of weather-gouged stone.

                    At times, it returned his breath.
          He'd risk touch of his lips, even ran
          his tongue tip along seams, heedless of stinging ants or
spiders that might lurk
          under sprigs of lichen or moss –
          he knew himself transported to past epochs
                    with old walls,
                              floors and warped or buckled roofs…
          until he stepped off a ridge
          into timelessness. He stood outside and above his stooped
figure, and watched
          millions of dribbles of water
          scoring tiny ruts and trenches in all surfaces,
    and each droplet left

                              its tinges. Faintest colorations.
          His eye learned to detect every shade
          or hue in the composite, and he embraced the weather-witch's
secret brew of color,
          refashioning Nature's slow-
          abraded mix of tints into his own palette
                    blend of oils.
                              His mental color code, taking fire
          from aeons of sun-baked crumblings,
          infused those yellowish shades into paint. And his passion
empowered the leggy
          beasties in climax of amours,
          propelling the Lady Mantis into a feral
    bloodthirsty finish.

Ras Akyem, *The Sins of Daniel*, 1995

THE GRANDEUR OF FOOT SOLES

"...and as the toes of the feet were part of iron, and part of clay,
so the kingdom shall be partly strong, and partly broken." (Daniel, II, 42)

All townsfolk who come
to see this portrait – I must understand – know the story it unfolds.
They've heard many versions of it, whether as youths
in Sunday School, or adults poring over their Bibles by late-night
guttered-down candles...

He prompts me
to read those few slices of speech –
inscribed graffiti – as sacred
clues, not to be scorned or written off by today's
hasty viewer as mere *toilet*
bleats, gutter scrawls. Observe MEATLESS DIET,
he says, engraved over the untouched
bowl of food at lower left corner of Daniel's
cell. Goat meat chunked
& rotting whole fish. Putrid or fresh,
'twas all the same to this man
of Visions, this truly clairvoyant
interpreter of Nebuchadnezzar's
dream – who offended and horrified
his accusers, if only because the dark secrets
he revealed proved to be accurate. His power
to see beyond such mendacities as
bound the Nobles to a realm of banal fact –
that they could never forgive... Here
we find Daniel caged in tall white-barred
crib, stowed in prison for refusing
to defile himself with the King's
meat. Thus, his *first* grave sin.
Encircled by various instruments
of torture. Hissing snakes dart
out at him

87

from above and below,
one now attacking his bare empurpled buttock. The fierce She Wolf
of *EMPYRE* glares down at him from a shelf – upper right –
poised to spring. Still uncowed, he defies the decree forbidding
him to pray at midday,

those few hours
reserved for the King's prayer only.

The Chaldean spies, eavesdropping
on his daily ritual and habit, tricked his friend
Darius into issuing the fatal

edict. Now he plainly has broken the ordinance
and will soon face the worst horror:
to be thrown into a lion's den. In these last

moments left to himself

his act of prayer rises to its highest

pitch. His *second* sin. For no

praying at noon shall go unpunished.

Of course, we know a miracle

will save him in that lion's dread

lair. It's a given. Home viewers have been briefed.
Local Barbadiana… Five feet high, four feet
wide, the lofty foreground is filled

with his stooped figure. Glarily lit upper
mid quadrant, a great space of turbulent
energies, is the square bounded by his gap-

toothed upturned face and heaven-ward
arched shoulders and arms, hands
and long tapered fingers woven around
upswung wrists in a human wreath:
his forearms twisted and bent upon
each other

like vines of wild ivy.
In his passion of search and prayer, he totally controls that charged
space, wide square of light bordered by his arms' sweet
self-embrace. If eternity can be bounded, encompassed, by man's act
of hugging the invisible

loveliness, Holy
Ghosts aswarm all about us, in and out

of Nature, this pictured embrace
gives it a radiant form. Noble and true, the accents.
To his captors, he would seem

to be hugging a void. But oh, it is the unseen
Beloved, the rich bounty of our days.
He vouchsafes an emblem – a shape – for rapture...

The green and purple bands
of those arm muscles and magically
exposed ligaments continue along
his naked back and sides, purply
globes of his buttocks modulated
to green across violet of thighs –
which calls up the shades of El Greco nightscapes...
The shock of his brown foot soles, *CLAY* stamped
on one heel, is the other locus of immense
color power. By an amazing mix of styles, Akyem
brings it off. From that surreal four-colored
amalgam of Daniel's face, pieced together in
jigsaw interlocking of squarish blocks –
red nose and forehead, orange eyes,
blue cheek and purple jaw – we are taken
by surprise, so true the bold shift
to realist exactitude in natural shaping
of those narrow

heels, each foot arch
curving into plump bulb of fore-sole and the lovely ovalesque rounds
of ten brown toe pads, individuated, one by one, singular
flowers in a fleshly bouquet. Likewise, that pendular brown sluglike
droop of penis, topped

by peacock-feather-
eye testicles (purple almonds enclosed

in brown sacks). But the foot soles
are piercing -- serene in their clarities. Now we know
we can love our bodies through

any travails. He has seen for us that neglected
glory of dull foot bottoms, as perhaps
no one before him... Such, then, be Daniel's most

grievous sins: fasting
& prayer, crimes aptly fitted to the King's
punishment. To be tossed -- raw
carcass feed -- to those lions... Counted
among his unguessed helpers,
note three stick-figure famous Persion

Kings, red-eyed & white-crowned, on plush carpet
of blue in the lower right corner -- peering down
at his feet, healing glances. Just below

their legs, two curved red bones, crisscrossed
to ward off evil spirits. A floor scattering
of fresh green-and-yellow peppers and scoured-

clean fish spines. Three surplus blue
crowns hover in air, above the white
crib bars -- offerings from the little kings,
a spare set for Daniel to place on
bare scalp, if he choose. *KROWNS & FAME*
incised above.

Ras Akyem, *Moses*, 1995

WHEN THE WATERS RETURNED

"And the waters returned, and covered the
chariots, and the horsemen, and all the host
of Pharaoh that came into the sea after them;
there remained not so much as one of them."
(Exodus, XIV, 28).

Dark-skinned Moses, a man of color –
crowned and bearded with loopy tubular design –
is seated. At leisure. So it seems,
for he contemplates his next moves in a chess game
with the Pharaoh. A White Knight,
emblazoned on his red robe front, stands victorious

beside the blank
square marked with an X from which Pharaoh's King
was toppled, his little black crown
knocked off
and pushed to one side. Pharaoh has been Check-
mated. Now Moses
clutches his serpent rod with both hands,
all ten fingers knottily intertwined
around this black staff which parts the Red Sea,
neatly, below his robes. But in the left panel,
long moments later, glint

formless red streaks
and smears amid a topsy-turvy
whirl of little boats and howling gape-jawed figures,
for those held-apart halves of sea now
sweep back, re-merging around Pharaoh's legions. Loose chariot

wheels are flying, while six drowning
soldiers tumble and somersault from side to side.
Big black fishhook, looped for a catch,
hangs above the green and blue medley of sea-and-sky
intermixed, the elements whipped
into such a frenzy the blurred horizon line's just

barely visible
between them. The dangled hook signifies *lure*
of magic pathway through the sea –
which drew
Pharaoh's army to give chase across the oddly
uncovered sea floor,
in pursuit of the fugitive Israelites.
The armies took the bait, and rushed
to embrace their massacre. The great Patriarch's
face is serene: his work is all cool laboring
with the Spirit. A passive

pose – meditation –
shrewdly conceals the huge effort
of his inner mind. Our man of God, half-mortal,
half-angel, directs that barbarous
scenario of upheaval in the left panel. His eyes seem to look

away, glancing to the side opposite
that havoc at sea, perhaps to fool his enemy –
throwing Pharaoh off guard. Those blue
and red geometric color blocks of his face composite
seem to match his flowing robes,
dark blue chair bottom and chair arms. His illusion

of quiet repose
so total, he may appear to dreamily nod off
                    into lulled absence. But his face
                    colors hide
          slow cunning of a chameleon: that false veneer
          a guise of laxity
     to befuddle his opponent... And Moses'
                    suavely chiseled hands, his knuckle-
creased fingers interlocked and moulded
                    like oaken logs around his long black cane, tell
          another story. The olive-

green pale glimmer
of his sculuturesque fingers, each
          gnarly digit carved to precise scale, looks eerily
          akin to the shades of yellow-green
          whirling across that tumult and roil-up of sea surface. Paint

                    colorist's key reveals that the agent
who wields those luminous appendages is the secret
                    mover behind the maelstrom of wind
          and waves... That viper head on his walking stick is no
               mere ornament or decoration,
     its long wicked tongue slithering out between two rows

          of white fangs.
A twin snake head, half-veiled at far left panel,
                    appears to preside over that melee
                    and fracas
          of typhoon which engulfs the Egyptian warriors.
               The airborne snake
          metes out havoc, punishments of the tempest:
                    a subaltern miracle-maker in the employ
of chief conjuror Moses, much as Ariel
               served Prospero. And Moses' red robes seem to flow,
          hauntingly, into the parted

waters of Red Sea
below his magic wand topped
      by the hissing snake head. Robes and sea wrack, too,
      seem conjoined in occult discourse:
      the master's cloak yet another agent of his sorcery. All messages

                  to be read into the portrait's color
code… In Akyem's *Moses*, racial or ethnic cross-
           overs are the norm in storied oils.
      Black Moses is Everyman, anytime, both then and now.
        Part human, part saintly, he's
   less one hero of legend than a vital oasis in our

        aggregate mortal
  soul. All of Nature – wind & waters, abyssal gulfs
            & rocky cliffs – conspires to bring off
              this miracle.
        We may all partake of the paint-embroidered weave.
        Who now enters
    the work's trance, and broods on its moves in
           and out of time, may be the Black Jew. Green-
fingered snake charmer. Crowned and bearded
      spirit Overlord who feigns idleness as he ever plots
    the collapse of empires.

Ras Akyem, *Nemesis II*, 1995

REQUIEM WITH TRUMPETING ELEPHANTS

I.

Rome is a shambles.
In foreground, dust has just cleared over the scene of carnage
and smashup. Receding behind the wrecked statues
and fallen pillars of grand marble buildings of State, many vistas
of action and setting —

roiled in tumult —
spin away in the distance.
They are cycles of time long past, but here
with us now, today.
All Rome came crashing down
in hours, mere minutes perhaps — monuments
levelled that had reigned
unmarred for a thousand years. Shatterproof.
Invulnerable. It was supposed. And least to be feared,
they fancied,
the scruffy invader whose conquests
abroad seemed tame

to the smug generals
and Heads of State. A man of the people, offspring of a family
of paupers — they mistook him for a crass lowlife,
paltry boor to be ignored. He might have been unschooled upstart
from their own slave

class — kept safely
underfoot, ever cringing.
All reports of his genius in battle, swiftly
pooh-poohed... Behold him

now. The Black Hannibal. Raven,
          in his lustrous black plumage. More vulture,
          while he surveys the spoils
outspread before him, wide-breasted and towering
over that carrion of enemy dead. Cheered by black and brown
               masked faces
          of his comrades-in-arms (one a cigar-
     smoker, his stogy

               adangle between rows
of glittering white teeth), gloating as they bob over the gutted
     ruins. Victory heads suspended, as if bodiless,
above wasted rubble of the fallen City State... Insouciant, regal
               blackbird! His broad

                    monumental torso
          stands erect on skinny black
               legs – those pronounced black testicles and penis
drooped down, hovering
          over two tall yellow mushrooms:
               the general's secret power fix? His long neck
          forward bent, his birdy
head is down-turned and leering in proud hauteur:
some few ruffled head feathers curling askew from his lowered
               scalp, one wing
          a bit bedraggled at the fringes – his sole
     visible hurts taken

               in surprise offensive
assault, wound up just moments ago: dust swirl and fracas still
     aflutter, variously, in that distant cityscape: right
panel... A white Roman head, gorgeously sculpted, lies at Hannibal's
               feet, blasted from one

96

time-honored statue,
a sprig of leaves still tucked
in its hair. That dazed blue eye, spookily
lifelike, is wide open –
stone crack running across the face.
A hybrid form perhaps, the truncated white
head blends flesh and stone,
traces of the human lurking around both hair
and nostrils. A fallen marble column has now come to rest
tumbled behind
the lopped-off head, its Corinthian
ornate crown topped by

fine acanthus leaves,
displaying the fastidious skills of the stone-smith. *Unfractured*
& doomed... The outsider, dubbed a mutant or retard
by the Emperor's scribes and sage advisors, jiffily swept away
all palace ramparts.

II.

Hannibal, bird-man of Carthage, looms up
tall – framed by jigsaw
composite of four primary color blocks: white,
yellow behind his ink-black head,
red and blue. An outlaw
on a Wanted Poster. His face –
mug shot of felon –
plugged into a police line-up, glares
in calm triumph over the puny collapsed

forces. World rulers for a Millennium.
                              Unchallenged. Till now...
                    Two souls in one, this bird soldier. Future
          and past merged in one puffed-out
                                        blackbird breast. Akyem,
                  today, veiled as Hannibal, hurls
                      his third-world
                                        challenge at the Post-Colonial White
          powers-that-be. His painterly gauntlet thrown

down, off the margins he leaps. And he'll
                                infiltrate the global-
                    art mainstream. Once within, he would topple
                  the pillars that quarantined him –
                                        hemmed into a far corner,
                  marginal man... The close-fitting
                      wedges of color
                                        that encompass Hannibal's physique
          a near-symmetric shield: it's wider at the top,

red-white-yellow, all red below, except
                                for white square inset
                  framing his low-hung black genitals. Bold
          colors, each a geometric chunk
                                        of quadrilateral shape,
              form an expanse of paint armor.
                      Rich thick-textured
                                        oils. An impasto buildup of layers.
          The medium itself speaks out. This black avenger,

White Racists' nemesis, brandishes
                            color shield impervious
              to attack. Sheer power and control of style,
          oils on a canvas, can be both
                            rock-solid art defense
          and brisk rounds of artillery.
                Unassailable.
                            Narrow streaks of red, yellow or blue
          underpaint, showing through Hannibal's black vest

of feathers, reveal his wounds. He's fully
                            mortal! Vulnerable
              in the flesh. But winged and feathered, since
          he's inhabited by an Angel's
                            Soul – half human, half
              divine. Those wounds aflicker
                    beneath his feather
                            cloak, the General's imposing tall stance
          dominates the left panel, his legs extending

below the bottom edge. His head, if not half-
                            bowed, would much overtop
              the canvas high border. And a few stark emblems
          decorate the wide tri-color
                            frame around his blackly-
              glistening body. The stick figure
                    bowman, poised behind
                            his wing, keeps arrow shaft in place –
          at the ready to defend his chief. A small white

crown, aloft, hangs suspended over his head.
                    That purply-black spade
            looms above the crown. Below, one lone elephant,
        a straggler from the right panel
                        chain of the expedition,
        flails his trunk wildly overhead –
                as if trumpeting
                        victory cries for resplendent Hannibal,
        whose ragged wing feathers nearly graze its tusks.

                            III.

Right diptych panel, equal half of the work's spread, is a fierce
            mix of marks and figures
    and items of graffiti text. *DEAD STONE*, printed in black
        over the decapitated marble head and downed
    column below. *CHARIOT*, crossed out between two loose wagon wheels
            floated above –
        the cancelled word evokes the horse-drawn vehicles
            absent from view, but smashed
                to smithereens:

those many horses all scared off, or trampled perhaps, by the row
            of four elephants incised
    as in a sculpturesque frieze and embossed in faint, low
        relief at the upper border... *B.C. 218* appears
    cordoned off in its own blue square, date of onset of the second
            Punic War, which
        peaked in Hannibal's foremost victory at the plains
            of Cannae the following year.
                Dark right panel,

for all its bustling medley of details, is shaded in a wide range
        of tans and browns, many half-
   tones, as against whole primary colors of left panel.
      A couple of tall ladders remain upright, both
   employed by the invading troops to scale City Walls: that total
        circumambient
      barrier… In the chaotic jumble, two more archers
        take aim at fuzzy targets;
           three blue-masked

faces of the aggressor's henchmen grimace their full sets of ivories;
        and a scattered lost trio
   of elephants, broken off from frieze-like caravan above,
      seem to wander about: double-tusked, trunks
   swung in all directions, only the center-most one at rest. Upper
       right, a single
      high column is left standing. What need to smash all
       public edifice, making a point
         of overkill,

since Hannibal, as we know, was honorific – not the gross barbarian
        history has often miscast
   him to be, who gave dignified burial to all enemy dead:
      weapons and insignias placed at their sides.
   Amid many fragments of words, lone letters, a whitish modern car
       peeps out – *TIN*,
      pale caption wittily engraved over the auto. Brave
       time-traveler from the artist's
         Barbados milieu…

CRUSH INTO THESE BLAKK FEET

I.

Soaring at heart,
dream kin they may be – Akyem and Basquiat –
though the pair never met: Ras Akyem's *ALTAR* both
Requiem for the Dead
and post-mortem revival of the Black
Haitian's sizzling raw art...
Three panels. A minimalist triptych
in black and white. Two finished versions. One, black-
on-white-backdrop, is the foremost.
The other (reduced
detail, more simplified), white-on-black. *See*
both. Keep looking at one, the other,
checking it out
feeling your way –
a bridge between them. For one may turn
the other inside out, as an X-ray reverses
our human body,
revealing to the doctor's eye strange
truth of hidden parts.
Black/White inversion – a comment on Race
(false dominance: who is on top, who now on bottom?) –
cannot be lost on the looker...
The three tall panels
are thickly white-oil-covered. They mimic
white walls of run-down city buildings
in slum backstreets

Ras Akyem, *Altar for Jean-Michel Basquiat* (middle panel of triptych), 1995

mostly ignored by police duos,
where eye-scalding
graffiti spreads like wild ivy vines across
sheets of stone. Bold
lettering travels at all angles,
unstoppable: words often misspelled, or crossed-

out and respelled
wrongly, some flickering with sparks
of defiance, genius, gutter jokes, true pain or
grief. Where they abound,
urban sabotage reeks, for it stinks
of entrails, fish rot
and gunpowder blent... Much white space
in all three panels is crammed with those gray no-color
scrawls, word parts that appear grooved,
dented or scraped
into textured white ooze with the pointy back
end of paint brush. Black under-painting
below the white
surface vaguely shows
through, but blank white space still dominates...
Cursory first glance at the tripartite work reveals
three black *SAMO* heads
upborne near the center of each paintscape.
Those heads, like shaman
masks at Carnival, are death skulls. Squarish
white eye-holes and sinister broad grins of white-toothed
grillwork loom over those narrow
black jaws. Each death
mask hovers in space, neckless, suspended
between two back columns of tombstone.
With Matisselike

spare economy, those fewest black
lines and bars
hint a full monument propped over the still-open
grave in each trio
installment. They comprise a trinity
that adds up to one altar: ghoulish faces bobbing

like exhumed mock-
skulls of the martyred hero; or risen
image of his undying soul – perhaps bidden, coaxed,
to ascension by the act
of drafting the art work: *MAGICIAN*
GURU SHAMAN   listed
at lower right, alongside that last
tomb column, exhales overtones of necromancy, witchcraft,
from the trancelike cast of square eyes
aglow in those dream-
stark heads. They could be Paleolithic faces
lifted intact from cave walls…
The altar piece
speaks to us, mostly,
in top-to-bottom sweeps. But each mask, becapped
with its floating halo or *KROWN* of thorns, shimmers
over those tombside
fragments which, in left-to-right progression
across the three panel
units, come to resemble – more and more –
a human frame: from hips to ankles! And these secondary
horizontal readings of triptych
are adroitly prompted
by a few crossover graffiti that span,
or overlap, the hinges between panels:
CRUSH INTO THESE

BLAKK FEET, followed by the form
of an actual man foot
in the L-shaped bottom of third left tombside,
mimicking the colossal
Stone-Foot-Of-Ramses. Man and monument
blent into a hybrid form at last, the whole series

building toward
this magical fusion – *hints of Basquiat's*
Resurrection flashing here... Two pairs of long
sinuous black bones
round out the scattered black patches
(oblongs, strips, and glary-eyed
jack-o'-lanterns), spaced over pervasive
white oil portraiture. And *SPARE PARTS* is deeply eteched
above that far left bone set, as if
to say: stray dug-up
bones of Basquiat's skeleton – femurs, upperleg
thigh bones they may be – are kept
in stock, salvaged
and at the ready
for use in art, like so many surplus car parts
stored up for repairs. Ras Akyem plies an old bone
kit for refashioning
broken lineaments of the honored dead –
his precursors, ancient
or modern... This fantasia compiles graphic
bio of the dead painter, rages to sum up his life story
and art with bare minimal images
or least word scraps.
The more random or accidental they look,
the more those hidden intensities shall
come streaking out...

Quite a plunge Ras takes into risky
format – his prior
best works aswirl with rich diversity of colors,
and crammed with a full
mosaic of textured detail. What cost
of Spirit to opt for wide sweeps of blanket WHITE.

II.

WORDS ARE STONES. Graffiti words keep filling the gaps and voids,
blanks, negative space. More
and more, scrawled words must carry
the missing weight –
paint mass of former blocks of color. The few streaks
of tint, bold hue, flare out
starkly, and hurl a challenge at the black-on-white field
that would drive the color items away
or send them diving down below white surface.
Under-layers of orange, green, red
keep peeping out,

here & there. Blunt naked colors may weigh like tarnish on young
black martyr's spirit, glares
of disrespect for the dead. Mostly,
Ras Akyem carries
that full burden to express multitudes in Blacks & Whites…
Perhaps three discrete sets
of offerings hang suspended, afloat, over each fractured
silhouette of black altar and tomb frame.
One little cluster of magic words and fine-line
amulets, per panel. Each set hovers
as if supported

on some invisible altar top: dream platter, shelflike, of unseen
hands. Offerings are held aloft,
        so many rich libations to be poured
for that teeming
Spirit... LEFT PANEL. The altar top presents a chess-board
                pattern of crisscrossing
lines, not unlike smaller line-mesh that mimes a wide grimace
of teeth in the *SAMO* skulls poised up high.
        Two chess pieces – knight & king – appear: perhaps
        Basquiat's knight has already trounced
cocksure White King

        since knight is propped squarely on board, king shoved offsides
                    to the left. The Haitian artist
          had won his end-game with America, just
                   before heroin
      overdose took him! That chess match replays his streetsmart
              agile moves to outwit
   most art dealers and gallery bosses in his New York heyday...
         MIDDLE PANEL. Five-petaled red flower,
      pinwheel-shaped, lolls on its stem. Happy blossom
        of the Resurrection, it strongly hints
            all *SAMO* heads –

transfixed above – be true ascendant face of the noble dead man.
VOODOO printed to the flower's
      right, an arrow below points across
black altar column
to A.D., orange under-coat showing through the white.
        These alphabets glimmer with
sparkles of some formula for raising the dead by Haitian
witchcraft, and bespeak promise of a saving
      afterlife for the martyred Ikon. Eerie nostalgias
      ripple back to childhood in his homeland...
Follow the arrow

across the panel break. Settle on that simplistic boat. Its one-
masted mini-sail puffed out
over a dugout shape seems to recall
old papyrus boats
sashaying down the Nile, slave ships of Middle Passage,
and those exile vessels
carrying Haitian boat people to America. *TO EAST* inscribed
above the tiny hull – sail back to your roots?
This miniscule craft, in turn, beckons overhead
to a little red car shaped like a child's
toy auto labeled

TIN, taking us full-throttle forward to our modern day. A vision
that sweeps with ease and grace
from ancient Egypt and the African
diaspora to both
artists' present moment: subject and maker of triptych...
RIGHT PANEL. Moving clockwise
from lower left, a card-deck Black Spade X'd out like some
word blocks. (Don't be fooled. Even Basquiat
confessed he often drew Xs or barred lines over
graffiti words to catch more notice –
never to delete,

cancel out, or correct, as a grammarian might.) That gamy spade
links up with the chess-board's
vanquished king, the spirit of gamesman-
ship a key motif
of both painters. Above the spade's inverted heartshape,
note a list of racial slur
words, common street epithets: *SPADE NEGROW NIGGA BLAKK*
A couple are crossed out, as if street thug
is trying to choose among them – checking them
off, one by one, to get it just right
for this occasion.

108

Alongside the list, find two dangled fishhooks atilt like lures
to catch some passing feeder,
                    completing the contents of altar three.
Copyright logo,
appended over the hooks, a most telling clue: our painter,
                    himself, now claims all rights
of purchase. The viewer who nips the hooks and takes the bait,
as one who thinks he knows the true social
          heft – or racial bite – of slur words, shall be fooled.
          Snared like a caught fish! By image power,
Akyem reowns them

                    for his key design and art mission. Language, that double-edged
                              sword, is twisted. The words
                    lose their sting, taking on positive
                              nuance – epithet
          or smudge now worn like badge of honor. Words of demeaning
                    poison become war cries
          to silence the abusers… A black square frame surrounds *TAR*
                    within the word *ALTAR* of the painting's
          title – center panel, bottom. And smears of black,
                    cagily faking sloppy or careless craft,
                              run like nosebleed

from the *TAR*-block down, as if dripping quick off canvas bottom,
exposing bright under-paint
          flecks of green. Streaks of whole color leap
out at the eye –
like random ink blots spattered on white backdrop. They steer
          the inquiring beholder's
search for meaning, answers to those riddles set in motion
by leading players in the picture bio…
          A gold-orange trio, running from diagonal corner
          to corner across the whole three-part
expanse, discloses

quiet personal message, or secret confession, from yours truly —
architect of the altar. Gold-
tinged mushrooms, below the Rastafarian's
witch-doctor list,
reveal his own leaning to hallucinogens, his debt to mind
expanders, a fraternal link
to his sadly *O-DEED* model. The diagonal gold sweep runs
through red-orange *TIN* car in mid-panel
upon the small gold crown, upper left, perhaps
reserved for his humble aspiring self,
a would-be Knight

following in his mentor's art glory path. If that slanted chain
of faint gold figures belongs
to Akyem's own private history, unfolding
here in Barbados
today, a mystery triangle of red emblems near the work's
center — like the Bermuda
Triangle at sea — may decode other puzzle parts. The red smear
under-named *SCAR*, its low point. High point,
one large red crown, above-named *KING PLEASURE*.
And the aforementioned five-petaled
red flower forms

isosceles mid-point. While *SCAR* gash marks out pains and wounds
of Basquiat's early dying,
flower and *KROWN* — taken together — radiate
hope of afterlife
sainthood. Or Kingly Resurrection. Altar piece is moulded,
then, both as elegy
tribute, and as maker Akyem's sacerdotal shaping of his three-
paneled Miracle. He would offer up
his paint flesh as ransom, placed on the altar
shelf of God's hand — to insure second
life for Basquiat.

110

III.   RAS ISHI:
   Soil Eyes

Ras Ishi, *Isolation*, 1995

MAROONED

I'm fooled by the tall turbaned, white-shirtjacked fellow,
bouncy in his white Nikes: an imposter who tries to pass
for the noted artist Ras Ishi... When Ishi does appear, shy

and wavering
in his glance, I just know I've
met him before. So elusive was
his face in the self-portrait *Isolation*, I
hardly knew I'd taken it in
until now. The man before me, in loose-
fitting caftan and spare sandals,
near-speechless at first, as I, throws
me back into the face-
silhouette at painting's center.
His living visage, at a glance,
gives me the key to reenter
the all-but-hidden dotted-line
features of a lonely tranced
Being on the free-floating cosmos. *Marooned*, he
says he is. Black artist in his island
element. Whoever he may be seems
a void, in need of filling. And here,
the space of himself is invaded
by sparkly points & slivers & jewels
of varicolored lights: glittering
tiny bodies – stars or planets
(a few satellites & meteors
among them perhaps): all those
celestial luminaries of night-
sky pageant

flow in and out of his dim-lit demeanor as if his flesh be
immaterial and transparent. Vast distances of outer space,
we come to feel, are filtered and woven into his palpable

vision. Austere
calm gaze reveals he's not squelched

by the invasive planetary masses,
nor robbed of his overt physiognomy – an exterior
crust of flesh and hair.

Rather, his transparency shows he can contain
this fiery and pulsing cosmos
in Mindscape. The eye he brings to his weave

of many colors is a prism:
it renders himself near-invisible

and rechannels the Heavens back
to us through his high cheeks,

wide forehead, angular facebones
and cadenced downward spiraling

of his dreadlocks, outlined in visibly dotted chain
lengths: much as portraits of Sagittarius

(centaur & archer), Capricorn
or Scorpio might be limned in semi-hidden
dotted silhouettes, chalk-drawn
by an astronomer to portray those starry

constellations. But here, the one
embracing figuration is Ishi's
own cheek-and-jawbone perimeters
and bedazzling loops or braids
of his dread ringlets. His hair-
locks and face

might be spun out of gaseous trails and spumes of light...
As we brood over the portrait, the fleshly outlines loom
close and recede in the distance, by turns. His features

                 may seem fixed
          in one plane, a mere two dimensions.

      Or they enter flux of unbounded
                space and time: layers and terraces of shadow
    and light, the many levels

                    moving between hair curls, sliding to & fro...
  This work seems totally porous,
                a barometer of the maker's Spirit. The base

 color of night sky, space
                        deeps, is a surface of textured
 blue-black with turquoise flashes
                  of underpaint showing through.
Solar, sidereal and lunar bodies
               (dots & diamonds & ministarfish
 shapes), wanly aglimmer, are drawn in reds, yellows,
           whites and pallid greens. But hinted purplish
 halos circle each star or planet,

             quavering in resonance with magenta-tinged
 patches on lips, under-eyes and lower
         hair bands in the emergent sculpted head.

   Is the near-submerged face portrait
            a lost soul, rudderless vessel
     awash in great sea of outer space?
        Or does Ishi contain & command
    the abyss of star clusters, man
       a guiding center

to galaxies – his emptiness filled with riches of jeweled
other worlds? Surprise gateway! He has voyaged from finding
himself lost to losing himself found, at a single cosmic leap.

Outdoorsman, a field worker, he's robbed
           of human features –
     his head
shovel-shaped, staring red-pupiled eyes
           below, white liplike
     gashes
above (pained mouth uprisen to release
           outcry?)… Humanoid
     twin
of a shovelhead shark!
                        BARB & THORNS.
           Gaunt black figure,
     locked
behind red cage mesh of barbwire and black
           thorn branches: he looms,
     raised
in relief over creamy white backdrop. Tall
           weed stalks – topped by
     seed pods
edged with many stickers – complete the zigzag
           fence weave that repulses
     hireling
from his land.
                    Isolation turns *home exile.*
           Those red strands of barbed
     wire run
horizontal across his face and dark torso.
           Barbs are red five-rayed
     stars, wide

Ras Ishi, *Barb & Thorns*, 1997

as his staring eye orbs: one long wire
            sweeping over his brow,
        another
curved above his head like a wide helmet's
            visor. All four wires
        traversing
his body seem to drip red trickles, streaks
            running down his lower
        face, chest
and belly – he has wounded himself, in repeated
            attempts to overleap high
        barrier.
Though blocked, irrevocably fenced out, he
            holds his ground – glaring
        at earth
he has tilled and harvested. *He'll never give
        way...*
                    Spatter of red drops,
        seepage
from his wounds, falls like rain. A blood
            drizzle between the wires.
        Defiant,
unswerving, he bides his time, seems to know
            his deliverance will come,
        as hinted
by the oval crown-of-thorns halo floating
            overhead (its rim nearly
        touching
upper border of canvas)... Flat-topped,
            his head-and-neck shovel
        is poised
to dig future tunnels below the barricade.

His three wide chest bands
    and longer
hip-and-thigh column are shield and plates
      of body armor. His stance
   not passive,
still less cowed or daunted...
                  Thorn branches
    and wider seed pods slant
   vertical –
all black stems crisscrossing the bloodied
      stark fence wires and lolling
   over ashen
white landscape. None of these are blood
      streaked, none have wounded
   outcast
man, his flesh torn only by starry barbs.
      Man and thorn stalks, black
   thistle
pods, appear on the same plane. Perhaps
      he's kindred to the family
   of weeds,
they, too, dispossessed, uprooted, flung
      from the garden, but holding
   their own
beside fence wires. Together, he and they
      stand firm to reclaim their
   earth plots.

WHIP TAIL OF THE ONE-EYED CHIEF

This motley quilt in oils,
　　weaving many large color blocks together, assembles
the whole West Indies colonial
　　narrative at a glance – *Four Hundred Years*.
　　　White, blue, red, yellow & black primary color quadrants
　　　　　are grooved and tucked
　　　　　　　into each other, while overhangs or
　　tag ends of paint-puzzle parts take in the slack. Like one curved
　　　　　segment of planet's surface,

　　　this interconnected patchwork
　　fragment can stand for the whole. All four borders
　　　are edges that divide and interrupt
　　ongoing portraits,
　　　　stories, figures that continue offstage
　　　　　　into beyond-canvas hinterland... The grand diptych
　　　　is nine feet wide, five feet high. Toothiness the commanding
　　　　　motif! And beyond the many fanged
　　snakes, wolf dog biting jaws and scoured-clean
　　human skulls (each sporting full sets of teeth), those hard-
edged color tracts are sandwiched
　　or layered by a closeknit webwork of toothlike
　　　margins... The great tall white-jacketed figure of the overseer,
magisterial, imposing, measures from top to bottom
of the right panel. At five

feet high, he's nearly life
size – a *virtual reality* primped-up field chief.
His right arm thrust outward, hand
   upraised issuing a halt (traffic cop
      directing streams of movers), his left arm is lowered
         at his side clutching
            the cedar yellow wood-stock handle
of his lengthy serpentining whip that curves up, down & across,
            traversing both wide panels.

   And truly the white whip tail
is the sole contiguous line unit that connects
   these various geometric oblongs,
which seem dispersed
      like so many separate continents or
         countries on the patchwork quilt of map. The recurrent
      emblems – ships, field workers, skulls, mushrooms, carrion-hung
         gallows, crucifixions, lizards, snakes,
churches and the tall overseer himself – may appear
to be juxtaposed, randomly, over the wide spread of dramatic
terrain. A grim narrative tale
      yearns to declare itself though interplay of images
      within and between many colored blocks… The story of *Middle Passage*
commences with a pair of three-masted schooners,
each voyaging in full sail

         across two central jagged
      rimmed polygons, one cloud-white, the other sea-blue.
Pain of the breakup of families,
      tearing and severance of bonds between kin
         fellows across the four centuries of diaspora, may guide

our witnessing eye
　　　　　　to expect chaos, not order. But despite
that raw swirl of figures – humans strung up on poles or arm-nailed
　　　　to forked tree limbs, time-polished

　　skulls, fish skeletons and array
of loose bones – the chain of images seems to move
　　in circles or waves like the undulations
of the field master's whip.
　　　　And chief's white gape-mouthed head, dangling
　　　　　　his long orangish pipe (wood matching the whip handle,
　　　　for length and color), which dominates the right panel of diptych,
　　　　　　is set off against and rivaled
by stoic black face of the lady cane-field worker
flourishing her wide-brimmed red hat, at center of left panel.
Two heads of near-equal size,
　　her figure is shrouded behind orange and white rhomboids,
　　bordered by disguised animal faces: open-jawed… But her face floats
above the mishmash of emblems, looking serene –
becalmed and biding her time.

　　　　That varied display of animals,
　　here and there, half-hidden in their color zones,
offer marginal asides. Most startling
　are the fork-tongued snake head jutting down
　　　from the whip handle, which appears to have drooled five
　　　　　big drops of venom;
　　　　　　　and the wolfish mad-dog head, wide-
　　jawed, affixed to tail end of the long whip: snake, wolf and chief
　　　　　all one-eyed, Cyclopsesque.

121

The only face endowed with two black
eyes, our lady cane-worker's... Enigmas, more cryptic,
   are yellow-gold fish with legs and curling
long animal tails;
      or the pair of red salamanders – one per
         panel – in opposite corners. Both fish and lizards,
      odd hybrids like aboriginal cave drawings or quirky Egyptian
         hieroglyphics, harken back to pre-
history. A rebuke to Europe's false illusion
of its Past as be-all and end-all of life in the colonies.
   Those salamanders, reputed to live
      through worst fire blaze, stand for slaves and tortured
      ex-slaves alike, survivors, too, of killing conditions. White human
skulls and fish-beast-composite skeletons, all
linked in the lower sector,

         follow curves of the supervisor's
long whip, mourning the countless deaths in its wake.
Both elegy for the dead (that trio
   of portraits of the red-skirted, white-bloused
      black woman crucified: her arm-skewered torsos arranged
         in a triangle spread
            over the upper canvas), and veiled hope
      for the future – release from bondage emblazoned in the wide-eyed
         stare of lady field hand...

Ras Ishi, *400 Years Remix*, 1995

SOIL EYES

Aftermath. Postscript
    to the sea voyages in chains.
        She, white-eyed now, is braced to push on
        through whatever impasse,
her fertility intact. Ennobled… The soil, her mainstay
during both the slave and ex-slave eras, this lady cane worker's
        face fills the low central third
        of canvas. Face of hardihood. Survivorship…
    It's the shimmering
      merciless blaze of those cane field
        conflagrations. An inferno of fiercest
        daylight. Sun whippings, unrelenting. A pained brightness,
agonizing glare

        to rival Van Gogh's sunflowers…
        A cream-white grid
    of crossed bars dominates all but uppermost black margin,
          that column of dirt-rich
  darks. Below, saving earth flecks
      peek out like black soil eyes from minute slits or cracks

in near-solid weave
    of crisscrossed white matrix.
      At first glimpse, it appears that intense
      heat and white-out light
of the fields must dizzy the midday workers into mobile
stupor, robotic swoon. But perhaps the red-hatted woman at bottom

center is dreaming this scene,
          its overbright vistas thumping in her brain
  like a racing pulse
      beat. And its all-but-smothering sheen
        is offset, held at bay by the black streaks,
         sparks, and dancerly whole figures surging upwards
from black underpaint

          layer below, asserting its pitch-
            dark lavalike
     ground heave. *The living torch of soil life. Everywhere*
              a self-replenishing manna
   in the souls of Black cane-field
         survivors... Three tiers of field hands are sketched out,

as if in ensemble
    rows. The middle series of six
      appear as white-garbed lookalike crew,
      just below the plain
white edifice of their church. Two ranks of black-suited
figures, lined-up above and below, flank the middle tier. Upper left,
      one immense black star
        trails a long black beam like a kite tail, dark
    star itself half-kite,
      half-crucifix, in shape. To its right,
        lolls white-ray-rimmed sun with scarlet core,
        singular red to match the red hat of our saintlike dreamer,
her wide hat brim a linked

series of nine small pyramids,
decorative ruffles
along the edge. In her trance, God and Work are sole
twin lodestars of cane-
balers' waking days. What they see,
they truly own. Pale two-chambered church. Quirky dancelike

moves of their fellows,
choreographed in the ritual
lockstep glide of chorus lines. Recurrent
image of field hands,
that classic emblem, seems patterned as in a woven quilt.
Right arm bent at elbow and raised, left arm bent and lowered, feet
outspread and turned as in dance
twirls… *Overlit intense blur! But her sight*
borne of dirt shrinks all
past wounds into this hale moment: black
crucifix star, white-rayed sun, ensemble of co-
workers in white or black attire. And she carries the torch
for whoever is to come.

AERIAL GEOGRAPHIES

I.

An aerial broad view of landscape, *High*
Chambers projects the country of his birth — homeland
Barbados — as if seen for the first time
from a space satellite hurtling, end over end, across
the upper stratosphere. If partly
a *Nature* painting, it's more a mindscape of the island

nation than Ishi's usual setting in oils.
 Satellite photos taken
    of earth from low regions of outer
       space — not far
       outside the planet's gravi-
    tational pull — best give
 a clue to his intended perspective.
And close-ups of particular land zones may suggest
 views from a low-flying
       aircraft. Either the near or distant
    overhead survey... But we mustn't be fooled by the way
       outlines of color blocks appear
       to resemble graphs and plots of land portrayed
          on colorized maps.

His love of the farmlands of childhood,
beautiful physiques of field workers and gardeners
          of both sexes, gorgeous colors of flowers,
       herb plants and food crops — all fecund in his early works —
          still feed his vision and guide
    his palette. But his line now works to define boundaries,

margins, borders. The old passion to mould flesh
  globes and arbor melons,
    or tubers, is fully reined in. Bold line –
      so dependable
      for truest renderings of actual
  organic forms –
  is held in check… There are nostalgias,
fleeting backlooks at both scenes of youth and early best
  paintings. (He calls such
      glimpses, secret retrievals, *screenings*.)
    Overall backdrop runs across a spectrum of reds, from topmost
    purples and the deep maroon
    of sunset, lightening by slow shifts down canvas
      to scarlets, vermilions,

                          orange and ochre-yellows at the bottom.
Though times of day or seasons are hinted, gradations
           suggest mood shifts of our conjuror, shaman
     maker performing his *black magic rituals*: those mind games
        behind the scenes. Separate blocks,
    here and there, are self-contained color fields. Two larger

black areas, he tells me, are *prodigal earth*:
  rich soil, decaying matter,
    humus – ready for new plantings. Love
      for work crews, farm
      folk, has been lavished upon all
    thick-textured inky blacks
  of these units. The middle long farm
acreage rectangle with white farm house annexed to barn
  at the center. Below,
    another farmscape: wide squarish block

with frontal face-shot of lady worker at bottom, red-hatted,
dangling white ribbons. Top left,
a small black unit – framed between two green whales –
contains the masked

secret woman of Ishi's dreams. The artist,
himself, is imaged by a small red-potted plant, humble
blue flower, no arrogance or self-inflation
here. That flower, in mid painting on a white upright block,
may signal to the mystery woman
above. These two are matched, for size and central placement.

The wide narrow rectangle, an intense cream-white
block, is a sugar cane field
just after cutting – that stick figure
a lone woman
cane picker under a blazing
hot sun: relentless,
beating down …Ah, even as he names,
labels, each land zone on that fake map of rural Barbados
he proclaims each color
tract a *High Chamber* of his own transported
psyche, receiving its mind boosts directly from the high Cosmos,
and we're swept back to the focus
of aerial photos, plus the vantage of outer space wide-
angle perspective.

II.

Many free-floating
    images, both within blocks and scooting
    between them, may be bits of matter drifting down
from starry sky like tiny meteorites.
And these are things that penetrate your mind as you work,
        paint, dream your art. Do you know,
they're as real, as heart-wrenching in their pathos,
as those abused
        fieldhands... And the big tip-off
to this stellar dimension,
half-mystic, half-sexual? Those scores of spermatazoa rollicking

                        upwards and across
            the color blocks, but mostly congested
        in dense red environs. The white umbrella caps
              of mushrooms, tucked in zone margins,
     are psychedelic toadstools which can be gathered like wild
           flowers from hideaway fringes
      of semi-desert like peyote drawn from aged cactus.
                They are the source
        of his Rastafarian mind leaps
           and soarings. No, not drugs
for abuse or disease addictions, but a true conduit to ascending

levels of spirit.

      The *High Chambers*, here, are elevated

      and transcendent states – a second map and separate

geography adjacent to those land

masses. On parallel planes. We move from quarter to quarter

         in the voyage across gulfs. Dope

from mushroom caps is never the goal, but slow steps

in brave process

      to higher mind. Those recurrent

images, scattered about

dual landscapes, carry the message. They may be personal icons or

                arbitrary random

          pictures that simply caught his fancy

       and intuitively hook up with other drawings.

            They do a dance over the paint field,

   and perhaps convey no meaning beyond that cryptic beauty

        of forms. Church bells, whales, sun,

     planets and flowering vines… Creeping between frames

            of color tracts

     are the many persistent scarabs:

           bell-like Egyptian beetles,

white-winged or black-winged, by turns. They're arranged in zigzag

trails, strange emblems
  or alphabets that tell a whole story
  like hieroglyphics; but their tale is contained
in those pictures, not spelled out.
Don't try to decipher them (they tease and mock his critics),
    but let them speak to our senses,
bombard our emotions. Note fine gridlike paint format
of thin crossed bars
    pervades the work; if we look close
at the weave of pattern,
it reminds us we witness nature, or landscape, at some removes. So

                    great a sacrifice,
          so pained it has been to forestall
      his genius to portray glories of human figures
              in nature – primal earthy woman
    viewed in gardens, his trademark classic pose. Today, he rages
          for a new scale of loveliness,
    non-European, non-Western. He finds he must bypass
              all proven beauties
      that don't harken back far enough
                to recover the Black man's
African genes. Ethnic DNA... Aboriginal cave glyphs may point a way.

OMNIVOROUS

Starve. The verb
has been reborn a noun... Hunger is

raised to the Nth power. Foodless
universe. No way to be fed. No smallest morsels
can be had. To not eat at all

is a fact, a stasis; it's a totally passive
state. He, the male sufferer, martyr
& saint in heroic Being Alive, *is* a Starve.

Emptiness, if uttermost

absolute, can become total fillup.
The passion for swallowing all

things which surround our body
in Starve... That variegated

many-toothed surface is mosaic
of fragments, color blocks which all appear

to interlock, chisel-edged. Oh, have they
eaten into each other? The grips

between shapes may be jaws clamped, each
to each – patchwork quilt leveling

out all segments as equal. Jigsaw puzzle

parts all on one plane. Flattened...

Slowly, we make out the man's
face in anguish: green, yellow

and white face plates fitted
together; red blots for eyes
and nostrils;

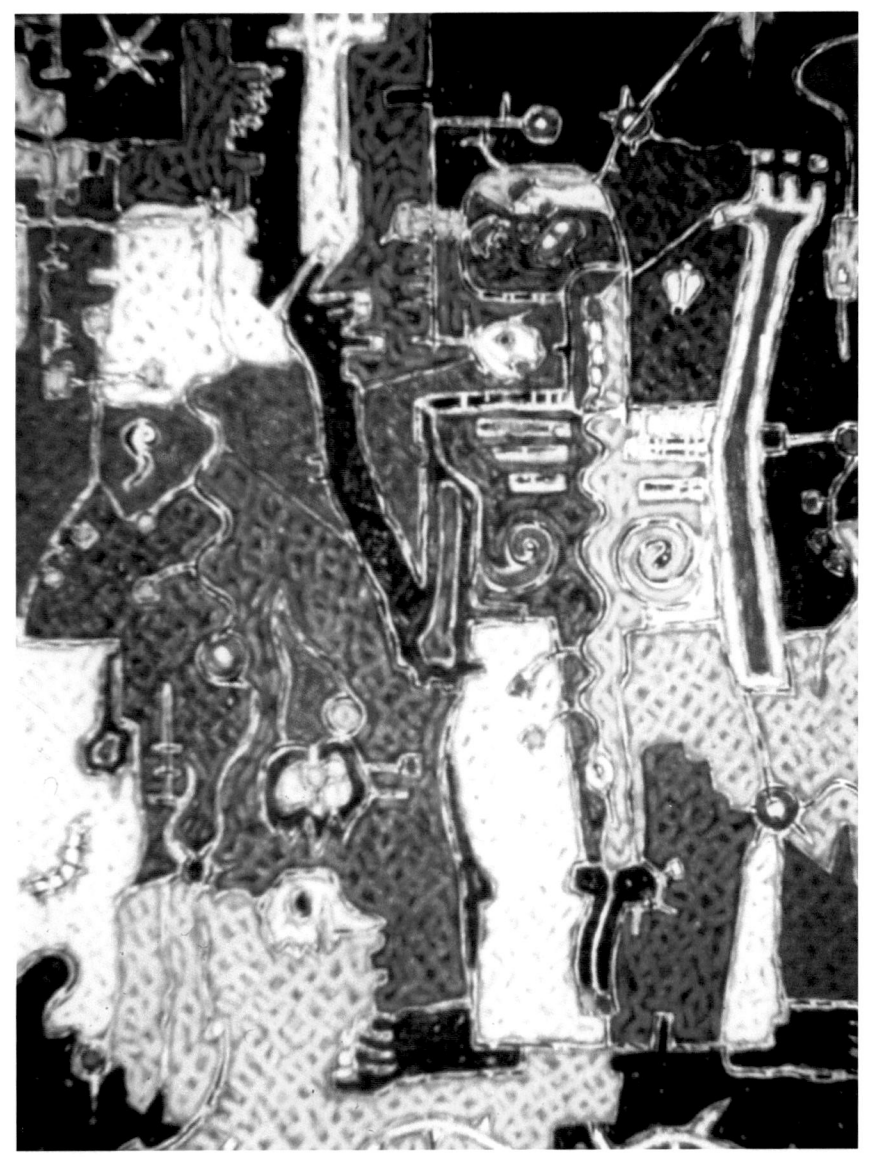

Ras Ishi, *Starve*, 1995

wider red gash for pained mouth agape under two front teeth
                                        intact, both uppers. We
        were fooled, we now see, by the seven colors
that aggregate to form the man's body shapes: they're almost

                        indistinguishable
            from similar mishmash of color zones

        throughout the lush pastoral scene.
                    But his head tossed to one side on the pillar
        of his neck, and his arm up-

                        raised in a spasm of grasping at plain air,
    are the giveaway. At first glimpse,
                        his figure was shrouded, lost to a viewer's

    eye, hidden in helter-
                                        skelter mélange of this portrait's
    map. True, the eye is helped
                                    by the dotted-line black margins
around his head & shoulders.
                                    But one red arm, white-bordered,
    threw us off the mark, temporarily blinded
                            to novel figure-ground relation, a unique
    interplay between man and environs.
                        His reaching out in appeal to those wide
        heavens – the Cosmos – is so intense
                        his body seems absorbed into a seamless
        webwork of all things. He becomes
                            invisible, whereupon ultimacy
                of starvation drives his body
                        cells to riot – then decompose
                and regenerate at once, as if
                        interwoven

                            133

with the landscape's embrace: plants and animals enveloping
                                                  him in their tentacular
        clasp. Look again. The fields seem to reverse.
Opposites change places. As the viewer's eye shifts, the scene

                        flipflops. Optical
            marvels abound... Now the landscape

        has invaded the man's whole body,
                    starting with green of flora in his midsection
        (chest and abdomen), and sluicing

                                upwards like fluids pumped by his heart beat
        into his lower face and jaws, then
                                down into one leg. But no, it's his body as

    aggressor sucking land

                                        & its organic issue into his limbs
    and flanks, as if arms or legs

                                        are straws through which he may
    quaff great draughts of fallow

                        surround. Supposed enfeeblement,
    or infirmity, now appears as occult strength.
                        A capaciousness of soul. Breadth of spirit
        akin to his upthrust arms, expanded

                            to limitless outreach. Starve long enough
        so bravely, and if you are not crushed
                            by gut aches, your emptiness contained

        bolsters your unknown quiet reserves.
                        A bulwark! You may be filled
            with unchewed gulps of vegetation
                        & rock formations alike, much
                as ostrich may swallow a stream
                    of small stones

while it gorges on earth. Material of your terrestrium becomes
$$\text{so much plenitude of grist}$$
for your digestive mill. Any common David may take
into his lifeline perimeters (body part outlines drawn in white)

the foliage-laden,
rock-stippled Goliath of his homeland…

Starve, the key to such omnivorous
feats. Our painter leaps into a novel realm, his
single haunted man a new species

of mammal. Background gives no depth behind
starver's physique. He seems flattened
upon those surfaces, his body engulfing all

portions of that near
landscape – he cannot depart from it,
nor return to it. Exterior
and interior vistas become alloyed.
Undifferentiated. Ah, it's
true psychic triumph for the man,
who witnesses his very flesh-and-bone turning
inseparable from its locale. This portrait
both grieves for his massive hunger

pangs, and celebrates his power to prevail
over them… Such juggling of figure
and ground opens a gateway to new freedom
in disposing the world with images.
A man's psyche may be depicted
as if it's composed of most things
he observes. For all the color
surprises here, blackness may rank
supreme—which

135

partakes of night sky, soil plots and core parts of the man's

                                       flesh. One arm, both feet
and his low-dangled genitals are starkly imaged
in solid blacks silhouetted with white borders. Long penis and

                        testicles, pendular,
               are drooped down nearly to the level

        of his two outthrust feet, all lobes
                   looking as fertile and moist as freshly dugup
     rutabagas. Those sky blacks, just

                  overhead (salted with tiny white star specks),
   like black earth patches immediately
                  underfoot, seem to be extrusions from wayward

  chunks of his anatomy,
                        a meandering fleshly corpus… Various
  broad color blocks enclose

                      insects, odd beasties, or half-hid
animal faces. The familiar

                 emblem of Egyptian scarab to one
side of his neck column. On the other side,
             a piranha head, gape-jawed as if puffed up
    to bite his shoulder; but exposed

            and picked-clean fish skeleton trailing far
   back from the face reveals that man
          or some other carnivore has beat it to first

    chomp (not he, surely, or he'd fail
           in purity of *Starve*)… One black-
     bordered orange butterfly, so near
       white caterpillar below red snail
     curled like a reverse question
      mark: harmless

trio to the arm-stretched pleader's left. But more intrigueful
                                        and ominous, we make out
            a half-veiled chicken's head – on the prowl perhaps
    (its large black eye in profile); and the perky cat's ears, white

                        on that earthy black
                    low border, the cat's body offstage,

            vanished below the man's right foot.
                    Gleamy six-rayed star or moon, pasted on black
            sky, balanced by the lower half

                            of gold planet running off uppermost canvas,
        above his agonized head linked to it
                            by magnetic white lines thin as spider-web

silks: brain rays! These
                                    appear to be trailing heavenwards
from the starving man's skull.

                                    A fiery cosmic charge, sending
its electric pulsings up and
                            down, fluoresces in the nerve

ganglions of his spinal cord and X-ray-lit tower
                        of four white neck vertebrae. Thus he makes
    cerebral contact with the numerous

                        astral or lunar bodies, which may provide
        the source of his supernal powers. They
                    are his dream and his succor. A soft answer

        to his prayers… Or is he, at last,
                    inconsolable? No moreso than plots
            of land that invade his unfended
                    transparent body. *Coterminous.*
            United, they mourn and exult,
                    as one flesh.

NOTES

I.   Works by Stanley Greaves

"Peas for Eldorado", after the sculpture, same title, 1993.
"Madonna with Pumpkin", after the painting, same title, 1998.
"The Neophyte", after the painting, same title, 2000.
"The Baxter Street Waltz", after the painting "Mrs. Baxter", 1992.
"The Maverick Hatter", after the painting "Hatman", 1992.
"Acuity", after the painting "Biscuity Story #1", 1991.
"Door Stoop Amours", after the painting "The Visitor", 1991.
"Fable of Mismatched Pairs", after the painting "Plantation Boots", 1991.
"School for Pancaking", after the painting "Mr. Facial, No. 2", 1992.
"Mapping the Sargasso City", after the painting "Prologue: There's A Meeting Here Tonight", 1994.
"Hour of Three Black Suns", after the painting "The Annunciation", 1993.
"Fable of Sky-borne Bananas", after the painting "Banana Manna #2", 1995.
"Magus with Reverse Bananas", after the painting, same title, 1995.
"Hour of the Mango Black Moon", after the painting "Morning Mangoes", 1989.

II.   Works by Ras Akyem Ramsey

"Ear Mug Handle", after the painting "King of Spades".
"Breath from the Mouths of Gloves", after the painting "Scarred", 1998.
"Moby at Ringside", after the painting "Moby Dick", 1998.
"A Taino's Burbly Hereafter", after the installation "Hatuey", 1996.
"Stick Paramours", after the painting "Mantis", 1995.
"The Grandeur of Foot Soles", after the painting "The Sins of Daniel", 1995.

"When the Waters Returned", after the painting "Moses", 1995.
"Requiem with Trumpeting Elephants", after the painting "Nemesis II", 1995.
"Crush into These Blakk Feet", after the painting "Altar for Jean-Michel Basquiat", 1995.

III.   Works by Ras Ishi Butcher

"Marooned", after the painting "Isolation", 1995.
"Shark at the Gate", after the painting "Barb and Thorns", 1997.
"Whip Tail of the One-eyed Chief", after the painting "400 Years remix", 1994.
"Soil Eyes", after the painting "400 Years Remix", 1995.
"Aerial Geographies", after the painting "High Chambers III", 1995.
"Omnivorous", after the painting "Starve", 1995.

ABOUT THE AUTHOR

Laurence Lieberman is a professor of English at the University of Illinois at Urbana-Champaign. He has published twelve collections of poetry and three volumes of literary essays. His poetry has appeared in *The New Yorker, Atlantic Monthly, American Poetry Review, Hudson Review, The New Republic, Sewanee Review, Kenyon Review, The Nation, Partisan Review, Paris Review, Boulevard, Southern Review, Colorado Review*, and many others. He has received the Jerome J. Shestack Prize awarded by *The American Poetry Review*, an NEA Fellowship, an Illinois Arts Council Fellowship and Grant, and a William Carlos Williams Citation from the Poetry Society of America. He has appeared in *The Best American Poetry*. Since 1971, he has served as poetry editor of the University of Illinois Press. His most recent book, *Flight From The Mother Stone*, appeared in 2000.

From reviews of his earlier books:

"In purpose and effect, Lieberman's writing is without boundary. Indeed, it's hard to name a more distinctive and original American poet writing today."
G. E. Murray, *Chicago Sun-Times*

"There aren't many American poets of any age who can synchronize elegance with spontaneity half so well as he. There is such a fullness to his art that our reading becomes as much an adventure as the voyage itself – breathless, invigorating, enlightening."
Publisher's Weekly.

"Among the few genuinely narrative American poets writing today, Lieberman is never likely to intrude on subject matter. His responsibility is to depiction, his inclination to describe.... The point of view is unique. This narrator gives the impression that he must assimilate everything and speak of it with the celebratory zeal of Walt Whitman."
Robert McDowell, *Hudson Review*